The CURIOUS and the CLASSIFIED

Praise for the Book

'A witty, informative and entertaining book which explores myths, mysteries, some lesser-known gems and the peculiar culture of the Indian armed forces. The evolution of quirky phrases and traditions is most interesting. The author and I belong to the same Regiment. For us, '*chak de phatte*' has been the most favourite and effective motivational chant in every competition. *The Curious and the Classified*, I am sure, will appeal to everyone; soldiers and civilians alike.'

General V.P. Malik (Retired)
Former Chief of the Army Staff

'General Manoj Naravane brings out both the heavy and light artillery to present military history with a human face. *The Curious and the Classified*, peppered with little-known facts and anecdotes engagingly recounted, once again proves that a Chief of Army Staff can be as much the master-storyteller as strategist.'

Bachi Karkaria
Columnist and author

'A witty, deeply informed and wonderfully accessible journey into the quirks, myths and living traditions of India's armed forces. *The Curious and the Classified* blends storytelling, history and humour to illuminate a world usually glimpsed only in salute and ceremony.'

Vikas Swarup
Former diplomat and bestselling author

'An utterly delightful journey through the 'aalis' and 'gullies' of Indian military history, picking up treasures along the way. General Naravane opens windows for us to peek through—smile at a Badluram or a Baba Harbhajan Singh or meander down Doolally without causing a SNAFU. The book introduces us to the ties that bind the Indian armed forces, his affection shining through at all times.'

Indrani Bagchi
CEO, Ananta Centre

'General Manoj Naravane has penned a delightful take on military quirks and idiosyncrasies and adeptly connected them with popular myths and beliefs. This book shows there is a lighter side to military life and retired Generals. A must-read.'

Nitin A. Gokhale
Author and national security analyst

'General Naravane's book is a masterclass in demystifying the Indian armed forces. With impressive literary craftsmanship, he weaves intriguing myths, mysteries and anecdotes, offering civilians a fascinating glimpse into the Indian military's ethos. It's an essential, entertaining read that is bound to bring the cantonment closer to civilian life. A truly captivating tribute to our forces.'

Happymon Jacob
Distinguished Visiting Professor, Shiv Nadar University
Founder & Director, Council for Strategic and Defense Research
Editor, *India's World*

The CURIOUS and the CLASSIFIED

Unearthing Military Myths and Mysteries

GENERAL MANOJ NARAVANE

RUPA

Published by
Rupa Publications India Pvt. Ltd 2026
161-B/4, Gulmohar House,
Yusuf Sarai Community Centre,
New Delhi 110049

Sales centres:
Bengaluru Chennai
Hyderabad Kolkata Mumbai

Illustrations: Simon Massey

P-ISBN: 978-93-7646-477-7
E-ISBN: 978-93-7646-646-7

First impression 2026

10 9 8 7 6 5 4 3 2 1

Printed in India

Dedicated to all soldiers, sailors and air warriors—whose quirks and foibles make these tales worthy of narration, capturing the customs, traditions and beliefs rooted in shared history that form the indestructible foundation of our Armed Forces.

Contents

SECTION III

WANDERLUST: MARCHING THROUGH HISTORY

SECTION IV

NOT ALL HEROES WEAR CAPES

SECTION V

WHO SKILLS, WINS

SECTION VI
TOAST TO TRADITION

Foreword

When General Manoj Naravane (Retired) reached out with the gracious request that I write the foreword for his new book, the first emotion that stirred within me was humility. Here was a man who had worn the nation's honour, carried the safety and security of our citizens on his able shoulders, had commanded the bravest of warriors—asking a storyteller for words. It felt like a blessing. It was a blessing.

Like millions of Indians, I have long admired the Indian armed forces as an institution of discipline, sacrifice and quiet heroism. And my admiration has always carried a special corner for General Naravane himself: a leader who is known for balance, measured courage, and a deep sense of *dharma*. To be asked by such a man to introduce his written work was an honour I accepted with gratitude—and, truth be told, a hint of trepidation. For I did not know what to expect from the General as an author. I knew him as a warrior and a statesman of the uniform, as a guardian of the Republic's frontiers. But as I turned the pages of this manuscript, I discovered delightful new facets of his personality: the subtle humourist, the keen observer of human nature, the patient chronicler of tradition, and the philosophical raconteur who remembers forgotten tales—and in his words, obscure military facts—hidden in a salute, in a mess rule, in a regimental story.

This book is full of charming nuggets. We have heard of the Molotov cocktail; but do you know about the Bangalore torpedo? Or that the origins of the salute may lie in Roman or Apache Indian protocol? Or how critical it is to return a salute? Or that 'dot on time' may be related to 'door opening time' of an aircraft? Or even why a Major is senior to a Lieutenant but a Major General is junior to a Lieutenant General? And one more—my favourite—that Mhow, our cantonment town, has a backronym—Military Headquarters of War! (Incidentally, I even discovered that a backronym is an existing word converted into an acronym.) Delightfully for an author, the General even finds the window in his tellings for the great novelist Jane Austen.

This book has been crafted by a soldier-scholar. In its pages, General Manoj Naravane opens a doorway into the world of the armed forces—soldiers, sailors and air warriors—through myths, rituals, jokes, toasts, and charming, heart-warming stories. He invites us to feel the weight of history in a badge of rank, the sacrifices infused in a regimental song, the touch of the sacred in legends like Jaswant Singh Rawat and Baba Harbhajan Singh, who stand guard upon our sacred geography even beyond death.

This book is aptly titled *The Curious and the Classified*—the 'curious' refers to the strange, almost unbelievable rituals and tales that are passed down through generations of officers, the unbelievable moments that soldiers remember. The 'classified' hints at those operations and experiences that remain officially secret, but live on in the lore of the forces. It is not just a collection of tales from India's armed forces, but a deep dive into the soul of the Indian military. Each story does not merely entertain but also highlights the core military ethos of discipline, sacrifice, camaraderie and *desh prem*.

Jai Hind! Jai Hind ki Sena!

Amish

Author, broadcaster and former diplomat

Introduction

In September 2024, I was at my friend Shailaja Nair's home in Gurugram. My wife, Veena, and she have been friends since their school days and over the years, Shailaja and I have become close friends too. It was her birthday and she had invited half-a-dozen couples over. Amid the ebb and flow of the afternoon's conversation, Veena pointed to a book on the centre table and asked if I had seen it.

She had apparently browsed it and found it intriguing. It was Shashi Tharoor's *A Wonderland of Words*. So I glanced at it, running my eye through a couple of paragraphs here and there. Then, not wanting to be unsociable, I reluctantly put it down. Reluctantly, because even in those brief moments it had captured my imagination. Afterwards, Veena ordered the book and, once it arrived, we were fighting for the privilege of reading it first. And I think it would be obvious who won!

At the time, I was giving finishing touches to my first novel, *The Cantonment Conspiracy*—a military thriller and murder mystery. Once it had gone for printing, my thoughts returned to *A Wonderland of Words*, which is a collection of essays centred around the idiosyncrasies of the English language. Humorous and informative by turns, it made for a delightful relaxing read—a welcome change from the serious, academically oriented non-fiction that populates usual reading lists. I might have earlier heard or read about some aspects covered in the book, but that hardly dulled the sheer pleasure of reading it.

It was the encounter with that book that set me thinking. If such a captivating book could be written on the quirks and peculiarities of the English language, how about a similar one about the Indian Army? The germ of this idea had popped up in my mind on the very first day when I looked at the book, but I could start thinking about it seriously only in mid-2025, after my excitement over the publication of my first book had somewhat subsided. With a tentative title of *Military Myths and Mysteries* in mind, I drafted a couple of chapters and showed them around. Rupa Publications responded with a strong go-ahead for the full-fledged manuscript. And so, from September 2024 to September 2025, it took a little over a year from ideation to manuscript submission. I unabashedly acknowledge *A Wonderland of Words* as the inspiration for this book.

With the idea taking shape, it was time to scout for stories. Each had to have something unique about it which would appeal to soldiers and civilians alike. There had to be an element of charm, of the unknown, perhaps even a touch of romance, as well as a large dollop of the many things taken for granted, which have deep historical roots. And the stories had to have their roots not just in ordinary history but specifically in the military past, culture and tradition, harking back to battles fought long ago whose legacy endures till this day. Each one needed to bind the past to the present, with a strong Indian connection.

I had a few such topics at my fingertips, though only about a half-dozen and not enough for a complete book. But they were adequate for sounding out family and friends, especially my erstwhile comrades-in-arms. And I was much enthused by their response to merely the gist of the story I planned to write. This almost universal appreciation and wonderment at my thinking aloud was hugely encouraging and also convinced me that I had latched on to an idea eminently worthy of a book.

However, what struck me most was that even some of my friends in the Army had not heard many of these stories. (Even seasoned veterans as well as historians among my readers might grudgingly admit that they did not know of some facet of a particular episode—or, going further, they may contest the version.) I found this strangely surprising, as I personally had taken most of these tales to be established military lore—gleaned during my many postings and varied travels. That they were known only to such few people spurred me to unearth more such hidden, less-known gems: stories that warm the heart, reaffirm our faith in the human spirit, and have their genesis in a military context. I am sure there are many more such myths and mysteries waiting to be unveiled.

I was also keen to have the tales appeal to the wider population, be anecdotal rather than academic, and yet have an underlying theme highlighting the military ethos. They could not be based on some obscure military facts buried in some dusty archive. They had to be closer to the surface in order to resonate with a wide readership through aspects the latter could identify with, possibly through frequent encountering though sans any knowledge of the historical background or importance. For instance, everyone has heard of Bangalore, and many live there or have visited this bustling metropolis. But how many have heard of the 'Bangalore Torpedo'? Torpedoes are used at sea, usually by submarines, so what is the connection with a city that is a thousand kilometres inland? Is there really a link with the city or is it just a name given on the spur of the moment? Similarly, is M.H.O.W. (Mhow) in Madhya Pradesh just another mofussil township (now renamed Dr Ambedkar Nagar) or is it the acronym for Military Headquarters of War? If not today, was it so in colonial times? Given that more than a few thousand officers and jawans are stationed at Mhow at any point in time (for training and as instructional staff), the latter interpretation has often been bandied about.

What is myth and what is reality? Sometimes the lines blur and it is difficult to tell. Stories that are oft repeated become the stuff of folklore. I have compiled twenty-five short essays, each dealing with a particular belief. Most of the stories are from the Army, but there are a couple from the Navy and Air Force too, in keeping with the spirit of jointmanship which is the flavour of the times.

All the stories have their origin in some real-life event, which, over a period of time, has got embellished through telling and retelling. The purpose of each story is to bring to life momentous events or characters, to bridge the gap between the Armed Forces and civilian society—while giving a glimpse into our world. There is no delving too deeply into historical accuracy. I may have taken certain liberties in this regard, to make each chapter more appealing, especially to a non-*fauji* (military) audience. In fact, many of the narratives themselves accord differing dates or interpretations to various events. At the end of the day, this is supposed to be an entertaining read and not a serious academic endeavour intended to be a competitive exam aid!

It was with this thought in mind that I wrote the first chapter, 'Chak De Phatte', and gave it to my friends and family for review. It is a phrase so commonly used, and in such a variety of circumstances, that very few know it has its origins in the heat of battle. Intrigued? Turn to that chapter and find out more. In fact, at one point of time I had even considered the phrase as an apt title for this book but dropped the idea in the interest of reaching out to a wider audience. Nevertheless, it remains my favourite chapter as it resonates deeply with the cavalier ethos of my Regiment, the Sikh Light Infantry. Which one is your favourite story? Do let me know.

Happy reading!

SECTION I

THE GRAMMAR OF UNIFORM

1

The Ladder of Life

Climbing one rung at a time

'Rank does not confer privilege or give power.
It imposes responsibility.'

—PETER DRUCKER

Few realize quite how faithfully the Armed Forces have embraced Drucker's words. After all, service personnel take their ranks very, very seriously, and not knowing the correct hierarchy or terminology has led to many a faux pas, not to mention an early end to promising careers. Add to this the fact that each of the Services—Army, Navy and Air Force—have their own terminologies, and you have a recipe for many a humour-in-uniform moment. Perhaps that is why service ranks have always confounded the vast majority of people worldwide, civilian and military personnel alike. These ranks have percolated down the ages and are almost uniformly followed by all armies in the world. This does make global interoperability much easier but is also reason enough to make us pause and wonder as to how this universal application evolved. Was it just an accident or does it have its roots in the colonial conquests of the past, a legacy which endures even today?[1]

But I may be jumping the gun here. Before going any further, a glance at the rank structure and equivalence is in order (from most junior to most senior). More so because many of these terms will occur later, so what better way to start than by introducing the service ranks!

ARMY	NAVY	AIR FORCE
2/Lieutenant*	Acting Sub-Lieutenant*	Pilot Officer*
Lieutenant	Sub-Lieutenant	Flying Officer
Captain	Lieutenant (IN)	Flight Lieutenant
Major	Lieutenant Commander	Squadron Leader
Lieutenant Colonel	Commander	Wing Commander
Colonel	Captain (IN)	Group Captain
Brigadier	Commodore	Air Commodore
Major General	Rear Admiral	Air Vice Marshal
Lieutenant General	Vice Admiral	Air Marshal
General	Admiral	Air Chief Marshal

The rank of Second Lieutenant (2/Lt and its equivalent) was done away with in the Indian Army, Navy and Air Force in 1997 as part of the Fifth Central Pay Commission, and officers now get directly commissioned into the rank of Lieutenant (or equivalent).[2] In earlier days, there existed a rank senior to

1 Strachan, Hew, *The Politics of the British Army*, Oxford University Press, 1997.

2 Ministry of Finance, Government of India, Report of the Fifth Central Pay Commission, January 1997, https://tinyurl.com/ymaxs637. Accessed on 3 November 2025.

that of General, namely Field Marshal, necessitated when the armies of many countries fought together as allies, each having a General at the helm. However, this and its equivalent in the Navy and Air Force are now only for ceremonial purposes. The Army has two—(late) Field Marshal K.M. Cariappa and (late) Field Marshal S.H.F.J. Manekshaw—and the Air Force has one in (late) Marshal of the Air Force Arjan Singh. Field Marshals never retire, so the suffix 'retired' is not used after their names. The naval equivalent is Admiral of the Fleet.

Seeing the table on page 4, it would be fair to ask as to why Lieutenants and Captains in the Navy write (IN) or Indian Navy after their rank. Well, it's not because they don't know which service they belong to, but to differentiate themselves from the same ranks in the Army, which are lower in the pecking order. As evident from the table, an (Army) Captain is quite junior to a Brigadier; a Lieutenant in the Navy is equivalent to an Army Captain; and a Navy Captain is equivalent to an Army Colonel, just one rung below Brigadier/Commodore. To simplify matters, many countries, including the US, use the Army ranks even for the Air Force, naming the service in brackets, viz. Colonel (Air Force).[3] The Navy continues to follow its own system, as do most navies worldwide.

The mismatch between the designations for various ranks often leads to inter-Services imbroglios. I recall one such incident when a Navy Commander was doing a course with the Army. In those days, mobiles had not yet made their appearance, and one had to book calls through the Army exchange. This naval officer would ring up and identify himself as Commander Kumar (name changed), and ask for his call to be put through, which was done quite expeditiously. During the course, he was promoted to the rank of Captain. But now, whenever he would call the exchange and say, with understandable gravitas, 'Captain Kumar, get me so and so number', he would be placed on hold interminably! For the operator, 'Commander' was the colloquialism for 'Brigade Commander' while 'Captain' was simply a very junior person who could jolly well wait. 'So how did you solve the problem,' I had asked the officer. 'Quite easily,' he replied. 'I started calling myself Colonel Kumar!' That was perhaps the first true example

3 U.S. Department of War, US Military Rank Insignia, https://tinyurl.com/23ut7x22. Accessed on 4 December 2025.

of inter-operability and tri-service synergy, much before the concept of theaterization had even raised its head. This is also why Lieutenants and Captains write (IN) after their ranks to clarify their Service and, more important, their seniority.

Little wonder then that civilians are always confused as to who they are dealing with, especially since the badges for each rank are a code in themselves. When one meets Service personnel, one should be able to read the rank from the insignia on the shoulders, name from the name tab above the right breast pocket, and the length of service and experience from the array of colourful ribbons above the left breast pocket. The colour of the uniform is indicative of the Service—olive green for the Army, white for the Navy and sky blue for the Air Force. In the Services, therefore, one does not need a visiting card, when all the details are right in front of you, waiting to be deciphered.

The great rank riddle

Inter-Services confusion apart, a question often asked is: If a Major is senior to a Lieutenant, why is a Major General junior to a Lieutenant General? There are many theories around this so-called anomaly. The first, most logical, explanation is that the prefix 'lieutenant' means a trusted adviser, usually someone next in line or a rung lower. Just as we have governors and lieutenant governors, we have the General (Chief of the Army Staff aka COAS) in command of the Army and a Lieutenant General (Vice Chief of the Army Staff aka VCOAS) as his number two. But how did the word lieutenant come about in the first place? It was probably derived from the French *lieu* (meaning 'place', as in the commonly used 'in lieu of') and the word 'tenant' (meaning 'holding', as in tenant an appointment). Thus, a lieutenant was literally someone who was temporarily acting in place of someone superior, in essence a deputy.[4]

Another theory traces its origin to the ranks in the British Army where the highest enlisted rank was that of Sergeant Major, senior to all the other Sergeants in that unit but junior to the most junior officer, viz. the Lieutenant. And therefore, you have (Sergeant) Major followed upwards in the pecking order by the (first) Lieutenant. This, in turn, explains why a Major General ranks below a Lieutenant General in the pecking order.[5] Over time, the rank of Major came to be added, just below a Lieutenant Colonel.

My preference is for the first theory, since we also have Lieutenant Colonels, junior to Colonels. In the Indian Army, a Colonel as the Commanding Officer (CO) commands Battalions or Regiments, as the case may be (and this distinction will be dealt with later), while his Second-in-Command (2iC) is a Lieutenant Colonel, ready to step up and take over should anything happen to the CO, especially on the battlefield. The 2iC, therefore, is supposed to know everything; but in practice no one tells him anything!

This situation, though seemingly humorous, highlights the dichotomy between the responsibility of the rank and the actual access to information. The 2iC's role is vital yet the CO often keeps all the crucial decisions to himself, leaving the 2iC in the dark on many issues. In fact, there is a popular military joke that the 2iC is the most senior officer without any responsibility. This underscores the awkward position of the Lieutenant Colonel, who, while mandated to step into the CO's shoes, is often not

---

4 Oxford English Dictionary, 'Lieutenant', OED Online, Oxford University Press, 2025, https://tinyurl.com/yftatyap. Accessed on 3 November 2025.

5 Holmes, Richard, *Redcoat: The British Soldier in the Age of Horse and Musket*, W.W. Norton & Company, 2002.

included in the decision-making process, especially in the heat of battle. This anomaly continues even at higher levels, not unlike the numerous vice presidents in big corporations who are often not in the decision-making loop.

Let me end with the Navy and give the last word to Jane Austen who used a light-hearted ditty on naval ranks to humorous effect when she cheekily referenced this pun in *Mansfield Park*: 'Of Rears and Vices, I saw enough. Now do not be suspecting me of a pun, I entreat.'[6]

And on that note, we part.

---

6 Austen, Jane, *Mansfield Park*, edited by R.W. Chapman, Oxford University Press, 1986.

2

Hats Off to Absurdity

Ranks and appointments: When the twain meet

The Army Training Command (ARTRAC), based in Shimla, has a specific branch to deal with our not-so-friendly neighbours. In that branch, officers of the rank of Colonel looking after Pakistan and China hold appointments called Colonel General Staff [Col. GS] (Pakistan) and Col. GS (China), respectively. As is typical in the Army, calls are booked through the telephone exchange where the operator has to be told who is calling and the number to be connected. A common ruse adopted by foreign intelligence agencies is to call up one of these exchanges, posing as an Army officer, and ask to be put through to a particular person or number. The exchange operators have been trained to be perpetually alert for such subterfuge and to disconnect immediately. Imagine the exchange operator's consternation when he answers a buzz—only to have the caller identify himself as Col. GS (Pak); his shock is equalled by the officer's bewilderment when he is abruptly disconnected, and repeatedly, without explanation. On each such occasion, the operator would report to his superiors a bid at a likely phishing attack by foreign intelligence operatives. Meanwhile, the officer would complain about the insolence of the operators from the Corps of Signals, the branch of the Army that deals with communications. Eventually, the confusion was sorted out and a simple solution found: the officers would identify themselves by rank and name only, and not by appointment.

This often-misunderstood—rather, not understood—differentiation between the rank (that one holds) and appointment (office one holds or job one performs) can lead to humorous situations like the one narrated. The Services have a penchant for tying themselves into knots by trying to cling to tradition at the cost of upward mobility.

Simply, ranks and appointments are two different entities altogether. While holding the same rank, an officer might serve in various appointments over the course of a number of years—until promoted or superannuated. A Colonel (rank) can be a Commanding Officer or CO (appointment) or hold any of a dozen other appointments such as Col. GS (Operations) [Ops] or Col. Administration (Col. Adm.). Further, an officer may also hold more than one appointment. The Chief of Defence Staff (CDS), for example, wears three hats—that of the CDS, Chairman of the Chiefs of Staff Committee (COSC) and Secretary of the Department of Military Affairs (DMA), each having their distinct roles and charter, with one 'hat', on occasion, perhaps overruling the others![1]

1 Integrated Defence Staff, Roles and Responsibilities of the Chief of Defence Staff, Department of Military Affairs Charter, 2020.

This interesting overlap of responsibilities is something I encountered as well. As a Company Commander in the rank of Major, I was not only the officiating Second-in-Command (2iC) of my unit, but also sometimes officiated as the CO in his absence. Often a jawan would be 'marched up' to me for disciplinary action, and having considered the merits of the case, I would either dismiss it or refer it for final disposal to the CO, who has the power to sentence offenders to imprisonment or other lesser punishments. The next day, I would sit in the CO's office and the same jawan would be marched up to me once again, but this time in my avatar as the CO, much to the consternation of the hapless jawan who had to face the ignominy of being 'marched up' twice.

The duality of rank and appointment is peculiar to the Armed Forces. In other government services, a person may be Shri/Shrimati Axx Kumar, Superintendent of Police (SP). When he or she gets posted or promoted, he becomes Shri/Shrimati Axx Kumar, Deputy Inspector General (DIG). Strictly speaking, SP or DIG are not ranks but appointments, although these organizations replicate the Army badges of rank, creating a false sense of equivalence. On retirement, he/she will become simply Shri/Shrimati Axx Kumar.

Service personnel, on the other hand, retain their ranks for life—as stipulated in Article 18 of the Constitution of India. Brigadier Axx Kumar, Commander, 33 Infantry Brigade, on retirement will relinquish the appointment (which someone else would have taken over) but will remain Brigadier Axx Kumar (Retd). Many organizations write Brigadier (Retd) Axx Kumar, which is incorrect. A simple way to remember the correct placement is that it is the officer who has retired, not the rank. In fact, to avoid confusion, the President's Secretariat has even issued a letter reemphasizing this.[2] Theoretically, an officer does not retire from these ranks and holds the most senior one till death; in effect, they are 'on duty' till their demise, even continuing to be subject to the Official Secrets Act, 1923, till the last breath.[3]

Of BMs, BCs and other vanishing ranks

Being 'on duty' for life is ingrained in us early on, as are several other aspects of military life. During our time in the Indian Military Academy, as part of our capsule on Service writing, we are tasked with writing a demi-official letter to the Brigade Major (BM) of a Brigade, making some request. A demi-official letter is written in a personal capacity but pertains to an official matter. These exercises were quite like school ones—write a letter to your uncle describing your summer holidays, and the like. Most of us, as yet ignorant of the Army hierarchy and appointments, addressed the officer with 'My dear Brigadier'. It turned out to be incorrect, because the BM is actually the appointment held by an officer of the rank of Major. An officer of the rank of Brigadier commands the Brigade—the Brigade Commander, colloquially known as 'Commander'. The BM is his Principal Staff Officer (PSO) who looks after operational matters.

Another piquant situation involving the BM arose when it was decided that this appointment should be upgraded vis-à-vis rank: from Major to Lieutenant Colonel (Lt Col.). The purists put their foot down: if the nomenclature was BM, how could

2 President's Secretariat, Government of India, 'Clarification on Use of Military Ranks Post-Retirement', Official Memorandum No. PR/SEC/ARMY/2017/04, 2017.

3 Government of India, Official Secrets Act, Act No. 19 of 1923, https://tinyurl.com/2x9rkzf4. Accessed on 4 November 2025.

it become Brigade Colonel? Ergo: BC? That, of course, carried an even more negative Punjabi connotation! Placing an officer in the higher rank and then calling him a Major amounted to even more of a put-down. Traditionally, Lt Cols in staff are called General Staff Officers Grade 1 (GSO-1). However, there are GSOs-1 at all levels, from Divisions to Army Headquarters (HQ), but they are not PSOs. Finally, it was decided that the BM would be called Brigade GSO-1 to indicate his exalted status as a PSO.[4] Much ado about nothing, but it goes to show how organizations often get bogged down in trivialities. By the way, I wonder how cadets start their salutations now.

Years later, this debate about ranks and appointments was thrown into perspective when I happened to be idly leafing through a book on military history—of the British Army—among the many in the extensive collection of my father, (late) Wing Commander M.S. Naravane (Retd). I spotted the sentence: 'The recently re-introduced rank of Brigadier.'[5] I was a comparatively junior officer then and what stayed with me was that ranks are merely functional requirements and not sacrosanct; just as in the Navy, Commodore, the equivalent of Brigadier, is considered more of an appointment.

So, while the officer commanding a Brigade is of the rank of Brigadier, which perfectly equates the rank and appointment, what would happen if one were to decide to upgrade Brigades to being commanded by Major Generals? How could one say, 'Maj. Gen. Axx Kumar, Brigade Commander', when Major Generals traditionally command Divisions (with each Division

---

4 Army Training Command, 'Designation of Brigade Major as GSO-1', ARTRAC Policy Note, 2003.

5 Heathcote, Tony, *The British Field Marshals 1736–1997: A Biographical Dictionary*, Pen & Sword Books, 1999.

comprising three or more Brigades)? Or, what if the rank of Brigadier were abolished?

As and when the Army transits to Integrated Battle Groups, these would be headed by Major Generals, and the dilemma of rank versus appointment sorted out.[6] The fate of the Brigadier rank remains uncertain, judging by media reports suggesting that the Army is seriously considering a proposal to do away with this rank altogether. In my view, it would be a step in the right direction.[7] It is indeed time to retire this rank, just as that of Second Lieutenant has been relegated to history, at least in our Army.

Two to tango

The Navy has its own take on the subject. Here, Captain is both rank as well as an appointment. As a young Lieutenant (IN), one may command a small minesweeper, a vessel used to clear mines from sea lanes. As the importance and class of the vessel rises, the command will escalate to Lieutenant Commanders, Commanders and Captains. However, irrespective of the rank held, the Commanding Officer is the 'Captain' of the ship. If a signal goes out that all Captains are to report to the Flag Officer, it refers to the ships' Captains and not all the Captains by rank in Colaba! While the bigger capital ships are commanded by Captains, the aircraft carriers—the pride of the Navy—are commanded by Commodores. However, they too are referred to as 'Captain'. More often than not, they wear the rank badges of

6 Ministry of Defence, Government of India, 'Integrated Battle Groups: Concept and Implementation', Defence Review Committee Report, 2021.

7 Pandit, Rajat, 'Officer cadre restructuring: Army mulls doing away with Brigadier rank', *The Times of India*, 17 July 2018, https://tinyurl.com/e8v955th. Accessed on 4 December 2025.

a Captain while in command to avoid any confusion. That is why the Navy has the concept of Commodore being an appointment from which one can drop to Captain, if required. In fact, some of the billets specify this aspect as 'Commodore (While Holding Appointment)'.[8]

This dropping down to the next lower rank happens pretty often in the Army due to the concept of acting ranks, which are granted for functional reasons. For example, if a unit is authorized six Majors and is posted only five, the most senior Captain can be promoted to the acting rank of Major, provided he or she has the minimum qualifying service. The minimum qualifying service differs for peace and field (border areas). These promotions are also known as field promotions and can be quite fleeting, with or without any increase in emoluments. In 1983, when my unit, 7 Sikh Light Infantry was in a peace station, I was promoted to the acting rank of Captain, having served the minimum qualifying period of three years. My monthly pay went up from a basic pay of ₹750 to ₹1,600, which was quite a substantial jump in those days—with a four-figure salary being something of an asset in the marriage market. I got married soon after.

These acting promotions, though, depend on the vacancies in that particular unit and not on the batch of officers commissioned in that year as a whole. It is not uncommon, therefore, to have an officer of a particular batch getting an acting rank in his unit and becoming senior to officers of earlier batches serving in different units. The latter now have to address the junior officer as 'sir' on account of his acting rank. However, these ups and downs are taken in one's stride with no hard feelings; in practice, each side addresses the other with 'sir' out of mutual respect. It can all be

---

8 Ministry of Defence, Government of India, 'Commodore (While Holding Appointment): Clarification Note', Naval Personnel Branch Circular, 2020.

quite confusing for an outsider, though. The bottom line is that ranks and egos are never allowed to come in the way of cordial relations. Ultimately it is the substantive rank that matters, which is determined by the date of commission/seniority.

A substantive rank is granted based on the number of total posts authorized for that rank and notified in the *Gazette of India*. Once promoted to a substantive rank, one cannot drop to the next lower rank. The Army is authorized approximately 15,000 officers of the rank of Major, a figure arrived at after totalling all the vacancies across units, HQ and establishments, as sanctioned by the Government of India.[9] This overall figure cannot be exceeded. However, for various reasons, the rank is never at full strength, thus opening the door to granting of acting ranks. When vacancies arise across multiple ranks, an officer could get promoted to the next rank as well but, once again, in an acting capacity. This is now not as common but was frequent during World War II, and also when there was rapid expansion of the Indian Army post-Independence.[10] My uncle, (late) Major General A.S. Naravane (Retd), when initially promoted to Major General was still holding the substantive rank of Lieutenant Colonel.[11]

Ranks are uncommon in civilian life. Most forms for collecting personal details, including those online, cater only for 'Mr', 'Mrs' or 'Ms', and sometimes 'Dr'. Rarely, if ever, is there a provision for entering anything else manually. While filling in such forms, once the name is filled, say, Major Keen Kumari, the system will by default record it and/or print it as

---

9 *Gazette of India*, 'Sanctioned Strength of Officer Ranks in the Indian Army', Ministry of Defence Notification No. 12/ARMY/MAJOR/2022, 2022.

10 Praval, K.C., *Indian Army After Independence*, Lancer International, 1993.

11 Naravane, A.S., Personal Papers and Correspondence, Family Archive, Pune, 1980–2005.

Mrs Major Keen Kumari. The staff at a hotel will breezily welcome you with a 'Good morning, Mrs Major', convinced they've got the name down pat. It's rather reminiscent of the character in *Catch-22*, whose father names him Major Major Major as a joke; the hapless chap goes on to join the Army and, when promoted to the rank of Major, becomes Major Major Major Major.[12] In Punjab, parents have a particular fondness for naming their children after Army ranks—for instance, Major Singh. So, while *Catch-22* is fiction, a Major Major Singh in the Indian Army is very much a possibility, as is Colonel Subedar Singh!

This distinction between rank and appointment is perhaps one of the most unique and confusing aspects of Services life, yet it remains the basis of military operations and smooth functioning. This two-track system allows the Armed Forces to remain flexible and adaptive, as officers take on varying roles while remaining in the same rank.

From Colonels holding various appointments to the complex hierarchy of the Brigadier, Major Generals and Lieutenant Generals, and the concept of *acting ranks*, the military world is rich with mostly humorous anecdotes arising out of the intricacy of this system. Whether it's a minor communication breakdown between the army telephone exchange and the Col. GS (Pak) or an officer being temporarily promoted and suddenly becoming senior to officers of earlier batches, the Armed Forces are a world unto themselves where tradition, hierarchy and humour abound. In the end, while *rank* and *appointment* may seem like irrelevant distractions, these small distinctions are the key to how militaries operate worldwide. It is a complex *nritya* between the two that keeps the system running smoothly, albeit with some humorous incidents along the way.

---

12 Heller, Joseph, *Catch-22*, Simon & Schuster, 1961.

3

'Jai Hind, Sir'

A salute to military life and culture

Saluting in the Armed Forces, universally recognized as symbols of respect, discipline and hierarchy, is one of the most ingrained and almost spontaneous acts that one encounters. So deeply ingrained, in fact, that it is as if the hand flashes up to the peak of the cap of its own volition. This gesture has profound historical roots, rich traditions, a range of meanings and significance in military culture, which retain relevance even in contemporary times. There are many theories regarding the origin of the military salute, but how much is fact or fiction is anybody's guess. Tracing the roots reveals an intriguing journey spanning centuries, encompassing ancient empires and medieval chivalry, as well as colonial legacies and modern-day battlefield etiquette.

One popular theory traces the salute back to ancient Rome, where soldiers would raise their right hand to demonstrate that they were unarmed and therefore not a threat. Displaying an empty hand implied that there was no offensive intent while at the same time conveying trust and mutual respect. In certain circumstances, it was also an acknowledgement of one's superior officer, which is what it signifies today.[1] However, among some

1 Keegan, John, *A History of Warfare*, Vintage Books, 1993.

American Indian tribes, especially the Apache, raising the hand upwards with the palm outward probably conveyed the same message, so it is difficult to attribute the modern salute solely to Roman customs.

However, the Roman salute, most often depicted in films and art, is a straight-arm gesture; but that too is supposed to be a myth, a figment of imagination, as ancient Romans didn't actually use this salute. The gesture was probably popularized by Renaissance-era paintings like the *Oath of the Horatii* by French artist Jacques-Louis David, now on display in the Louvre in Paris. Completed in 1785, the painting shows three brothers from the Horatii family saluting three swords held aloft by their father, while the women behind him mourn. In this powerful moment, the brothers pledge their loyalty to the city of Rome. Coming just before the French Revolution, the painting won wide acclaim and popularity as it resonated with the revolutionary idea of loyalty to the state rather than to a monarch. This gesture was later adopted in Hollywood films like *Ben-Hur* and *Spartacus*.

Roman gladiators, facing their final battles, are said to have saluted the emperor with the morbid expression '*Ave Caesar! Morituri te salutant*' (Hail Caesar! We who are about to die salute you), weapons in hand. This straight-arm salute, though, was adopted by fascist regimes in the 20th century, by Italy under Benito Mussolini and Germany under Adolf Hitler, to evoke pretensions of imperial grandeur. This association with authoritarian regimes has since made the gesture controversial and distasteful, even illegal.[2]

Another probable theory traces its roots to the medieval period of knights in their shining armour. During this period,

2 Mosse, George L., *The Image of Man: The Creation of Modern Masculinity*, Oxford University Press, 1996.

knights would raise the visors of their helmets to expose their faces as a means of identifying themselves. This gesture not only brought the hand level with the eyes, but also naturally turned the palm outward. Try this with the plexiglass visor of today's crash helmets, and you will get the same results. This ritual of uncovering the face was a gesture of both respect and trust, as it exposed a chink in the armour. Once again, while this practice may indeed have been in vogue, there is little direct evidence to link it to the origin of the modern-day salute. Some historians feel that this explanation emerged from fertile minds keen to give the salute a romantic and chivalric aura, rather than being based on documented proof.[3]

The formalization of the modern military salute can more likely be linked to the 16th and 17th centuries when European military forces adopted more structured ranks and protocols. This necessitated the introduction of the salute as a universal practice, tied to the need for standardized norms within increasingly formalized armies, often fighting side by side. Another significant milestone in the history of saluting was the rise of professional standing armies funded by the state, as against conscript levies owing allegiance to feudal lords. As military organizations became more complex and hierarchical, the salute served as an important distinction of the relationship between officers and enlisted personnel, and between officers not only of different ranks but also of differing seniority within the same rank.[4]

Thus, the salute is much more than an empty gesture. It

---

3 Hanson, Victor Davis, *Carnage and Culture: Landmark Battles in the Rise of Western Power*, Anchor Books, 2002.

4 Lynn, John A., *Battle: A History of Combat and Culture*, Westview Press, 2003.

is a profoundly significant part of military life and culture. Its importance lies in its embodiment of respect, hierarchy, tradition and unity. When a junior salutes his senior, in effect he is saying, 'I acknowledge your authority and will follow your every command, even at peril to my life.' In turn, every salute must be 'returned' with the senior's saluting of his junior implying, 'I respect you for your commitment and shall never let you down.' It is thus an unspoken covenant that runs through the entire military hierarchy built on trust and mutual respect.

Ignoring or not returning a salute is a serious lack of form. There is the oft-quoted story of Field Marshal Manekshaw once noticing that a young officer had neglected to return a salute. In his own inimitable style, he asked the officer to remain where he was and return the salute of every jawan who walked past, thus disciplining him yet maintaining his *izzat*, and driving home the point that every salute is earned and is not to be taken for granted.[5]

The unspoken covenant: From real to reel

The act of saluting is an important tradition, but personnel from the Army, Navy and Air Force salute differently. This difference in the way the salute is executed by the three Services is also rooted in historical lore, romanticized traditions, unique service customs, and practical considerations related to the specific environments in which each Service operates.

5 Singh, Depinder, *Field Marshal Sam Manekshaw: Soldiering with Dignity*, Natraj Publishers, 2002.

The Army's salute is perhaps the most universally recognized. The salute is performed with the right hand, raised to the forehead, palm facing outward, fingers extended and the elbow bent at a 90-degree angle. It probably evolved as an amalgamation of folklore, fact and fiction.

In the Navy, the salute is distinctively different: it is executed with the right hand, palm facing down, and the fingers extended, but the hand is raised to the forehead at a slight angle. The Navy salute is often described as a more horizontal or angled gesture, where the palm is not visible, compared to the Army salute. This variation is ascribed to a couple of stories that make for good reading. Sailors on board ships often worked with ropes, sails and machinery which left their hands soiled or greasy. It is said that they saluted with their palm facing downwards to avoid offending their superior officers. However, there is no concrete historical evidence to suggest that the intention behind the angled hand was to hide dirty palms from view.[6]

6 Till, Geoffrey, *Seapower: A Guide for the Twenty-First Century*, Routledge, 2009.

Another charming version is that Queen Victoria was once visiting a warship. The Admiral saluted in this manner (he may indeed have had dirty palms!). On being asked why, he replied in all seriousness, 'To shield my eyes from the dazzling beauty of Her Majesty.' The remark is sometimes attributed to Vice-Admiral Sir John Jervis, who was later made the Earl of St. Vincent in honour of his victory at the Battle of Cape St. Vincent in 1797. The Admiral was reputed not only for his military acumen but also for his dry wit and humour. Whether his promotion was on account of his military acumen or his witty, exaggerated admiration of Her Majesty is open to conjecture. On a practical level, though, this form of the salute would definitely have shielded the sailor's eyes from the glare of sunlight reflecting off the water, particularly when the salute had to be held in position for extended periods as when compliments are exchanged while ships pass each other. While the palm-down salute itself had practical reasons, these apocryphal stories add a dash of humour and charm to the traditions of naval saluting![7]

In the Air Force, the salute is distinct again—with the right hand, palm angled upward and fingers extended, but the arm is kept at a slightly lower angle compared to the Army's salute. The Air Force salute is typically performed with the arm raised at approximately a 45-degree angle to the body. The origins of the Air Force salute can be ascribed to the evolution of air warfare, which developed only in the early 20th century. During the early days of aviation, pilots would salute from within the cramped confines of their aircraft, using a hand gesture that was visible both inside and outside the cockpit. This may

7 Rodger, N.A.M., *The Command of the Ocean: A Naval History of Britain, 1649–1815*, Penguin Books, 2005.

have influenced the angle of the salute. The 45-degree angle is also said to be evocative of an aircraft taking off, representing ascent and progress—but that is perhaps another case of reverse engineering!

Of the three Services, the explanation of the origin of the Air Force salute bears the best scrutiny.[8] Another crucial difference is that in the Army, one only salutes if wearing headgear, be it a beret or a peak cap. However, the other two Services salute even without headgear, once again probably because of their relatively cramped working conditions.

The act of saluting is also often accompanied by a verbal greeting, something that was introduced by the French during the colonial period of our history, particularly among the Sikh and Maratha forces. A salute accompanied by a cry of 'Sat Sri Akal' or 'Ram Ram, Sahib' was quite common and over time this custom became standard practice across all Regiments of the Indian Army. Amongst officers, it would be accompanied by a formal 'Good morning / afternoon / evening, sir', depending on the time of day. It was the Air Force which first started the practice of saying 'Jai Hind', which had neither any regimental connotations nor was it time-specific. At first, it sounded strange to our (Army) ears—long accustomed to the regimental greeting—but, over time, 'Jai Hind', has become the accepted salutation.[9]

A 'salute', however, should not be mistaken for a 'salaam'. While both are gestures of respect, they differ in their origins, cultural contexts and intended meanings. The former is rooted in

---

8 Boyne, Walter J., *The Influence of Air Power upon History*, Pelican Publishing, 2003.

9 First coined by Chempakaraman Pillai in 1907 and popularized by Netaji Subhas Chandra Bose as the slogan for the Indian National Army.

martial traditions and codified in military protocols. A military salute is delivered with shoulders squared, while looking the dignitary in the eye, without any bowing or scraping. It is a two-way exchange of trust and respect. On the other hand, a salaam (from the Arabic *salām*, meaning 'peace') is a broader cultural and religious greeting. It is commonly used in Islamic societies and South Asian cultures to convey peace, goodwill and reverence. The physical gesture of a 'salaam' often involves a slight bow, eyes down, with the right hand placed on the forehead or chest, a gesture of deference and sometimes subservience. Interestingly, in South Asia, especially in India and Pakistan, the term 'salaam' is sometimes used in lieu of the salute in informal settings, especially when making respectful gestures toward elders or dignitaries as in 'Salaam, Sahib'. But technically, they serve different purposes and come from distinct traditions.[10]

Perhaps it is this visual distinction that is frequently overlooked in popular culture. Movies often take creative liberties with military salutes. In many films, actors salute with a limp wrist, fingers spread or the hand too far from the forehead. A proper salute requires a straight hand, fingers together, and the tip of the forefinger just above the eyebrow—precision matters. Think of Alec Guinness in *The Bridge on the River Kwai*; he may be wearing a tattered peak cap, but his salute is absolute regulation. Yet, some Hollywood movies also depict over-the-top salutes, with exaggerated arm swings or theatrical pauses. While it may look cinematic, it is far from regulation. There is also the 'forehead tap' salute, with the hand barely flicking the forehead, often used for dramatic effect but lacking the

---

10 Ahmed, Akbar S., *Living Islam: From Samarkand to Stornoway*, Penguin Books, 1994.

discipline and respect the gesture is meant to convey; it leaves most military personnel exclaiming in disdain that watching military scenes in war movies is a test of tolerance.[11]

In contrast, saluting in Bollywood movies often carries deep emotional and symbolic weight. It's not just a gesture but a symbolic and climactic moment. Films like *Shershaah*, *Uri: The Surgical Strike* and *Sam Bahadur* showcase salutes as part of dramatic climaxes, often accompanied by swelling music, slow-motion shots and patriotic dialogue. The salute becomes a visual symbol for sacrifice and national pride. Actors like Vicky Kaushal and Sidharth Malhotra have portrayed real-life officers with a strong emphasis on authenticity, to evoke feelings of nationalism and patriotism. Their salutes, though often given to creative liberty, are nevertheless respectful. Bollywood also tends to blend realism with reverence. While the salute may not always be technically perfect, it's delivered with emotional intensity. On occasions like Kargil Vijay Diwas, actors publicly salute soldiers on social media, reinforcing the gesture's cultural significance beyond the military domain.[12] So, while both industries use saluting to convey respect, Bollywood uses it for sentimental reasons to do with resonance and national pride, whereas Hollywood switches between technical realism and making the narrative more purposeful.

Clearly, the salute has transcended its military origins. Nowadays, when I am out for my morning walk, I am sometimes greeted by fellow walkers or by the security guards. Touching the bill of my golf cap, I always respond with a 'Jai Hind'. It has

---

11 Grossman, Dave, *On Killing: The Psychological Cost of Learning to Kill in War and Society*, Back Bay Books, 2009.

12 Gokulsing, K. Moti, and Wimal Dissanayake, *Indian Popular Cinema: A Narrative of Cultural Change*, Trentham Books, 2004.

taken time, but after the passage of about a year, the guards all greet me with a loud 'Jai Hind, sir', sometimes even throwing in a snappy salute. On such occasions, I return their salutes and greetings, and it feels as if I'm back in the Army again!

Jai Hind!

4

Dot on Time

Because even seconds matter

'Early is on time, on time is late, and late is unacceptable!'

This is more than just a saying in the Army; it's a way of life which underscores the weightage accorded to punctuality. But this obsession with arriving early can often become a major irritant for military families, especially when heading for social events where nobody ever comes on time. I remember going to a wedding once. My wife and I reached precisely at the appointed time, but for the next hour or so, it was only us and the waiters!

Such experiences reaffirm quite how deeply the military mind is obsessed with time and time management. The day begins with the sounding of the Reveille at dawn and from then on, until the Retreat is sounded at dusk, each minute of the day is accounted for. Punctuality is revered, not just as a whim, but because it can be a matter of life and death. Precise coordinated actions by various echelons, mounted and dismounted, in the air or at sea, sometimes operating in different time zones, are essential for military efficacy and safety. For example, if an attack is scheduled for a specific time, everyone must be ready to go into action at that precise moment for the operation to succeed. Time is a key part of discipline, playing a crucial role in military training and operations. And in any situation when everything happens with military precision, it is described as 'dot on time'.[1]

How this term originated, or whether it bears any connection to the Armed Forces, is uncertain. 'On time' itself means that something has happened or is scheduled to happen at a specified moment or within an expected time frame, give or take a few minutes. A train lumbering into the station is 'on time' as long as it enters the platform and comes to a halt more or less as scheduled; a minute here or there is acceptable. The addition of the word 'dot', though, places emphasis on precision—literally or figuratively. It suggests that the event or action took place precisely at the given time, with not even a second's delay.

This emphasis on timeliness was likely an outcome of technological developments. In the era of horse-drawn carriages, to say that the stage-coach was expected to arrive by early

1 *Oxford English Dictionary*, Oxford University Press, 2025.

afternoon, meaning anytime between 2 and 4 p.m., would have been perfectly acceptable. With the advent of trains and aeroplanes, such a broad time frame could no longer meet the requirements of tight scheduling in restricted spaces. An arrival (or departure) time of 2 p.m. meant precisely that. As the world became more interconnected and schedules became more complex over different time zones, precision in timing gained in value. This would likely have contributed to the metaphorical use of 'dot' to convey an even greater degree of precision than merely 'on time', just like the 'dot' on top of the letter i.[2]

Military precision extends to even seconds, which are factored in during planning and execution. An artillery barrage, for example, might be laid down by different types of guns with different 'times of flight' for their shells, from the time they are fired to the time they hit the intended target. In order to engineer surprise, the ordnance from different guns must land on the target at the same time to achieve first-salvo effectiveness. If the time (duration) of flight for one type of gun/equipment is sixty seconds and for another thirty seconds, and the shells are to land on the target at 20:00 hours, then the first set of guns will fire at 19:59:00 and the other at 19:59:30 so that the whole salvo strikes simultaneously. (Because thirty seconds is long enough for the enemy to scamper to the safety of reinforced bunkers from the moment the first shell lands.)[3]

The Republic Day Parade held in New Delhi every 26 January affords another fine example of perfect coordination. From the moment the parade commander's vehicle starts rolling along Kartavya Path to when the last aircraft executes

---

2 Landes, David S., *Revolution in Time: Clocks and the Making of the Modern World,* Harvard University Press, 2000.

3 Bidwell, Shelford, and Dominick Graham, *Fire-Power: The British Army Weapons & Theories of War 1904–1945*, Allen & Unwin, 1982.

its 'vertical Charlie', every minute is choreographed down to the split second. In 2017, as the General Officer Commanding, Delhi Area, I was the parade commander and my heart was in my mouth for the entire duration of the ceremonies and spectacle. This was particularly because the pageant comprises not only marching contingents, but also boys and girls forming part of their school or college groups and dancing troupes, as well as the various state tableaux—all of whom have to be lined up and released in a precise order.

This split-second coordination is particularly true of the flypast where aircraft have to take off from different airfields, hundreds of kilometres apart, and then fly in a holding pattern until instructed to join the 'air-stream'. The slower moving helicopters and transport aircraft are released first, followed by the fighters. The timings have to be precise or the faster aircraft, if released too early, will swiftly close the gap—leading to inadequate separation and a potentially unsafe situation. On the other hand, if released too late, there will be long gaps or pauses between formations. As one formation disappears over the horizon, the second formation should have reached the saluting dais in the centre of Kartavya Path, and the third should be making its appearance over the dome of Rashtrapati Bhavan. The degree of precision and calculations involved can only be imagined, considering that speeds could vary from 200 kmph for helicopters to 500 kmph for transport aircraft and a breathtaking 1,000 kmph or more for the fighters![4] Notwithstanding the nerve-wracking coordination, rolling down Kartavya Path, under the gaze of a billion-plus fellow Indians, is an experience both humbling and unforgettable.

---

4 Ministry of Defence, Government of India, 'Republic Day Parade: Standard Operating Procedures', 2017.

Precision opens the door

Another interesting connotation of 'dot' is Door Opening Time (DOT). Often used in modern-day parlance, especially in the aviation sector, it refers to the exact time the door of the aircraft is opened, which may be several minutes after the aircraft has actually landed or come to a complete halt in its designated bay. Once again, a few minutes here or there may not mean much for commercial services, but timing is of vital importance when matters of protocol are involved.[5]

When a head of state or similar high-ranking dignitary is to visit, certain protocols have to be followed at the airport—such as the welcome accorded at the foot of the ramp stairs by senior representatives of the host country, the giving of a guard of honour, some sort of welcoming ceremony, perhaps a traditional dance performance, and the like. In other words, the proverbial red-carpet treatment. However, due to safety reasons, all these arrangements cannot be made until the aircraft has come to a halt. Once the engines are shut down, there is a flurry of activity. The red carpet is rolled out, the waiting VIPs escorted from the lounge to the tarmac, and the artistes lined up. Simultaneously, the troops for the guard of honour march up and a portable dais is placed for the visiting dignitary to take the salute. All this takes time; and the visitor remains onboard, perhaps even observing this flurry of activity or getting a last-minute briefing about the dignitaries in the reception committee or of the procedure to be followed for the guard of honour. It is only when all arrangements are complete that a message is passed to the captain of the aircraft who then gives the orders

---

5 International Civil Aviation Organization, Manual on the Regulation of International Air Transport, ICAO, 2021.

to the crew to open the door—on the dot of time. This is how crucial DOT is! [6]

While 'dot on time' and DOT share a common emphasis on precision and timing, they are hardly related—having differing origins and applications. 'Dot on time' is a general expression used colloquially to denote punctuality to a highly precise degree, often in the context of business, social events, or personal interactions; DOT, in contrast, is a protocol-specific term that refers to the exact time a door opens in certain situations.

Though there may be some conceptual overlaps between the two, since both terms emphasize precision and exact timing, there is no evidence of any direct historical or linguistic connection between the two. DOT emerged from the practical needs of transportation systems, while 'dot on time' likely evolved from broader cultural trends that increasingly valued punctuality.[7] However, both terms illustrate our societal obsession with time and the growing importance of precision in an increasingly fast-paced world. Thus, while the two expressions share a similar focus, the differences in usage, context and historical development suggest that this connection is purely coincidental. Nonetheless, both terms highlight the critical role of punctuality in modern life, whether it's opening a door on time or showing up to an event at the given time, something that is becoming increasingly rare in an age when arriving 'fashionably late' is the new status symbol.[8]

---

6 Ministry of External Affairs, Government of India, Protocol Handbook for State Visits, 2022.

7 Zerubavel, Eviatar, *The Seven Day Circle: The History and Meaning of the Week*, University of Chicago Press, 1985.

8 Levine, Robert, *A Geography of Time: The Temporal Misadventures of a Social Psychologist*, Basic Books, 1997.

5

Long Story Short

Decoding abbreviations and acronyms

Abbreviations and acronyms have been part of military communication, whether written or spoken, much before becoming a fad in the present era of Short Message Service (SMS) and WhatsApp chats. Unlike civvy street where such abbreviations emerge as a result of popular local usage, those in the Armed Forces are a standardized set of abbreviations and acronyms for words and phrases that are most frequently used. There is actually an entire manual, one of the many an officer has to study during training, devoted to them. Titled—what else but *Abbreviations*—it contains thousands of words and their authorized abbreviations, which have to be used mandatorily in all Service communication. Appropriately enough, the first entry is the abbreviation for abbreviation: abvn, plural: abvns!

The usage of abvns in military (mil) communications (comns) was born of operational (op) necessity, to be able to pass messages (msgs) quickly and efficiently (eff) in the shortest possible time. The abvn msg [the reader has to interpret the tense and part of speech depending on context] itself acted as a simple code which would not make sense if it fell into the hands of an enemy (en) not conversant with it. Some, like CO for Commanding Officer or LC for Line of Control, are now well known even outside mil circles, while others like ETA or estimated time of arrival (arr) and ETD or estimated time of departure (dep) have, among many others, entered the civilian (civ) lexicon. Quirky abvns like 2iC for Second-in-Command and kmi2h (km in two hours) continue to amuse everyone even as they are the forerunners of many such absurd-sounding abvns used in contemporary chat parlance that combine numerals and letters.[1]

The ABC of mil comns are Accuracy, Brevity and Clarity. Ancient armies, such as the Roman legions, were known for their disciplined (discp) comn systems (sys). Roman soldiers used shorthand notations to mark (mk) orders, troop (tp) movements (movs), and msgs that needed prompt dispatch. However, it wasn't until the advent of written mil records, and the subsequent administrative (adm) burden, that abvns truly flourished in mil contexts.

With the advent of modern technologies (techs) such as wireless radio telephony (RT), radios, satellite (satl) comns, and digital msg sys, the need for quick, eff comns became even more crucial. The fast-paced, dynamic character of modern warfare (W), with its high-stakes ops and constant real-time exchanges (exchs) of information (info), while denying the same to the en, demanded sys that could deliver (del) info in as little time and with as little effort as possible.[2]

The requirement (reqmt) for brevity became a singularity of the era of comns using the Morse code, where each letter of the alphabet is represented by a series of dots and dashes. It owes

1 Chatterjee, Sabyasachi, *Military Communication Systems: Evolution and Practice*, KW Publishers, 2018.

2 Roy, Kaushik, *War, Culture and Society in Early Modern South Asia, 1740-1849*, Routledge, 2011.

its origin to the need for a faster method of long-distance (dist) comn than traditional methods like messengers or semaphore and was developed by Samuel Morse and Alfred Vail in the 1800s as part of their work on the electrical telegraph. The initial code focused on transmitting numerals but was expanded to include letters and punctuation. Morse code revolutionized long-dist comn, enabling faster and more eff info exch across dists, and paved the way for future comn techs.[3]

Yet, each word had to be transmitted in full, which was time-consuming. Short to medium (med) gaps between transmission (txns) indicated when a new letter, word or sentence was beginning. The word 'message', for example, would get transmitted as - -/. / ... / ... / .- / --. /., a total of fifteen txns with six gaps (/), whereas the abvn 'msg' would be much faster - -/... /--. with only seven txns and two gaps, thereby decreasing the overall txn time by almost 50 per cent. One can imagine how invaluable abvns became in the era of the Morse code and the equally important need for standardization (std) of both the code and the auth abvns.

Common punctuation marks (mks) also had their own code, but using them increased the length of the txn. It was, therefore, better to draft msgs that were simple, easy to understand and quicker to transmit. Since there were no separate codes for capital letters, they were done away with altogether, though a procedure does exist to indicate capitals—but that only increases (incrs) the length of the txn and so is best avoided. Training (trg) of operators (oprs) became all-important (imp). The modern trend of not using capital letters at all, even at the beginning of sentences, originated

3 Standage, Tom, *The Victorian Internet: The Remarkable Story of the Telegraph and the Nineteenth Century's On-line Pioneers*, Walker and Company, 1998.

from this. It assumed even more importance with the advent of electronic warfare (EW), when the adversary would scan the airwaves, home in on txns and eavesdrop on the conversations (convs). It was the tech equivalent of catching a messenger alive.[4] The shorter the msg, the less the chances of interception.

Swearing by the alphabet

Now, acronyms too have their own tale to tell. While those like CO are quite common, there are many longer and colourful ones. It is an interesting pastime to figure out what the full form of an acronym could be in its mil context. The proliferation of acronyms has become so rampant that one wonders whether it's a boon or a bane, especially as anyone not part of the sys is rendered perplexed. Often, the acronym itself has been used for so long that even the people tossing it around casually have forgotten its full form! This is equally true of all professions that have their own specialized jargon. Most people, including bureaucrats, would be hard-pressed to give the full form of NITI in NITI Aayog or MGNREGA (now proposed to be renamed as VB-G RAM G).

Some acronyms have become so intrinsically part of vocabulary that they are used as normal words. RADAR, which stands for radio detection and ranging (rg), was invented in the United Kingdom during World War II. This electronic equipment (eqpt), which allowed England to track (tr) incoming German bombers, was a turning point (pt) in the Battle of Britain—the air war between England and Germany. Its underwater equivalent was SONAR—sound navigation (nav)

4 Deshpande, Meera, *Behind the Uniform: Personal Lives of Indian Soldiers*, Orient BlackSwan, 2019.

and rg. Modern versions of these wartime inventions are in widespread use today. Nowadays, radar is used in civ contexts to describe anything that is being tracked or monitored, whether in aviation, meteorology, or even in everyday speech—e.g., 'I'm not sure what's going on with her, she's not on my radar.'[5]

D-Day is another mil term that is widely used. The term D-Day was first used by the US mil sometime in 1918 during the closing stages (stgs) of World War I. It was a generic mil term used to designate the day on which a particular op or event was set to take place, most commonly a mil landing (ldg) or offensive. 'D' simply stood for day, so D-Day expanded becomes 'day-day', which does not really make sense but nevertheless conveys urgency and importance. The term was used as part of a broader system for planning (plg) ops, without setting a specific date (dt) in advance (adv) for the op to be launched. All other activities and events were in relation to 'D'; D minus 10 meant something that should take place ten days prior to 'D' as and when that dt was finalized, whereas D plus 10 would mean ten days after the launch of the op. The term, though in use off and on, actually became part of modern folklore during World War II, on 6 June 1944—the D-Day of the Normandy landings or the Allied invasion of France which marked the beginning of the end of World War II.[6]

Nowadays, D-Day is used casually in many convs and, over time, the term has taken on a more general (gen) meaning, often used symbolically to denote any major (maj) high-stakes event or turning pt. For example, an expectant mother might

---

5 Price, Alfred, *Instruments of Darkness: The History of Electronic Warfare, 1939–1945*, Pen & Sword Books, 2005.

6 Ambrose, Stephen E., *D-Day June 6, 1944: The Climactic Battle of World War II*, Simon & Schuster, 1994.

be asked, 'When is the D-Day?', meaning 'delivery (del) day'. In other civ settings, it might be 'Tomorrow is the D-Day for our project—the final presentation (psn).' Or 'It's the D-Day of our product launch.' In these contexts, D-Day no longer strictly refers (ref) to a mil event but to any pivotal moment that would change (chg) our fortunes. In civ life, the use of D-Day may sound incongruous, but its connection to events that have changed the course of history lends it a heft that few other terms can match. It serves as both a reminder of the past and a call to action for those facing their own challenges, whether personal or professional.

Many acronyms are now used in everyday language, often with a slightly altered meaning or tone, but still bearing their mil roots. From logistical (lgs) terms to battle field (fd) slang, these abvns are now part of the fabric of everyday comn in civ street.

Let's take a look at some of the most commonly used mil abvns that have made their way into the broader civ lexicon.

- AWOL: Absent without leave. AWOL refs to a Services member who has left his or her post without permission or authorization (auth). It is a serious offence and could result in disciplinary (discp) action or court-martial. In civ life, AWOL has become a casual (cas) way to describe someone who is unexpectedly absent or missing without explanation. It's often used in a humorous or light-hearted context, as when someone fails to show up to an event or appointment (appt) without explanation.[7]

7 *Oxford English Dictionary*, Oxford University Press, 2025.

- SNAFU: Situation normal, all f***ed up. A humorous albeit crude way to describe a situation that has not gone as planned. Most mil plans don't survive the first shot, nothing ever goes as planned, and hence the ironic 'situation normal, all f**ed up!'[8] The Sikh Light Infantry version is even more colourful.
- FUBAR: F***ed up beyond all recognition. The big brother of SNAFU, this is mil slang used colloquially to describe a situation (sit) that is irreparably broken or beyond repair. It's often used to describe missions (msns), ops, or eqpt failures that have gone horribly wrong, even in civ life. 'The plans for the weekend are totally FUBAR. It's raining cats and dogs, and the car won't start.'[9] An example of this is Op Eagle Claw launched by the US in April 1980 to rescue its citizens being held hostage in Tehran, requiring a complex chain of refuelling and flight (flt) ops deep inside Iranian territory. A severe sandstorm further complicated matters, rendering a number of helicopters (heptrs) unserviceable. A collision between a heptr and a C-130 aircraft (ac) caused several deaths in the rescue party and the msn had to be aborted with no hostages rescued. Classic FUBAR.[10]

---

8 Partridge, Eric, *A Dictionary of Slang and Unconventional English*, Routledge, 2002.

9 Lighter, Jonathan E., *Random House Historical Dictionary of American Slang*, Random House, 1994.

10 'Operation Eagle Claw', *Britannica Online Encyclopedia*, Encyclopædia Britannica, https://tinyurl.com/rustwxzs. Accessed on 4 December 2025.

- MIA: Missing in action. Ref to mil personnel (pers) who are unaccounted for after a battle or msn, and their status unknown. After KIA—killed in action—it is one of the most dreaded terms since it leaves the future uncertain, filled with hope and dread simultaneously. In civ life, MIA is used to describe someone who has disappeared or is unexpectedly absent from a sit. It can ref to anything from a person not responding to messages to someone who's just vanished without a trace as in dropped off the radar.[11]
- SOP: Standard (std) operating procedure. In the mil,

11 US Department of Defense, *Military Personnel Status Report,* DoD Publications, 2020.

an SOP ref to a set of established (estb) guidelines or procedures that outline how certain tasks should be carried out, ensuring consistency and eff. The term has entered the civ lexicon to describe any std or estb procedure in various industries—whether in corporate settings, health (hlth) care, or customer service. It's often used to emphasize routine or protocol.[12]

- PTSD: Post-traumatic stress disorder. It is a mental hlth condition that can develop after someone has experienced or witnessed traumatic events, particularly in combat (comb). It is a serious issue that affects many veterans. While PTSD originated in the mil, it has since been widely adopted to describe anyone suffering from the mental and emotional aftermath of a traumatic experience, whether related to an accident, abuse or other distressing life events.[13]
- IED: Improvised explosive (expl) device. An IED is a home-made bomb typically used by insurgents (insurgs) or non-state actors in warfare, designed to target (tgt) mil pers or civs. It has become a signature (sign) weapon (wpn) in modern asymmetric W. In civ life, IED is sometimes used figuratively to describe an unexpected, expl and destructive event, particularly one that causes turmoil or a significant tremor in the system. 'The budget cuts were like an IED—we didn't see them coming, and now the company is in turmoil.'[14]

---

12 Katz, Daniel, and Robert L. Kahn, *The Social Psychology of Organizations*, Wiley, 1978.

13 American Psychiatric Association, *Diagnostic and Statistical Manual of Mental Disorders: DSM-5*, APA, 2013.

14 'Improvised Explosive Devices (IEDs)', GlobalSecurity.org. Accessed 2021.

- CYA: Cover your a**e. CYA is widely used to describe actions taken to protect oneself from blame, especially when something is likely to go wrong. It is about ensuring that you have documented (docu) or prep yourself against any SNAFU. CYA has made its way into office culture, especially in corporate or bureaucratic settings. It refs to any effort made to save one's skin, often by docu decisions, taking cautious steps and ensuring everything is on record or signed off by a superior.[15]
- UXO: Unexploded ordnance. UXO refers to bombs, shells or other ordnance (ord) that have been deployed (dply) but failed to detonate (det) as intended, often leaving them as a dangerous hazard. In civ use, UXO is sometimes used figuratively to describe any unresolved or dangerous sit that has been left unaddressed for long and could cause problems in the future. 'This problem we're dealing with at work is like a UXO—it's going to expl in our faces if we don't deal with it soon.'[16]

Are abvns a boon or a bane? The answer lies in bal. When used appropriately, abvns are a boon, enabling faster DM and more eff ops. But when overused or misapplied, they can become a bane, creating confusion and hindering comn. The key lies in context, std and trg, ensuring that abvns serve as a tool for eff comn without sacrificing clarity or comprehension.

If you have been able to read this last para without any problem, hats off to you!

---

15 Bennett, William J., *The Book of Virtues: A Treasury of Great Moral Stories*, Simon & Schuster, 1993.

16 International Committee of the Red Cross, 'Unexploded Ordnance and Humanitarian Risk', ICRC Reports, 2019.

SECTION II

SIGN, SYMBOL, STORY

6

Bangalore Torpedo

Mines, malt and the Madras Sappers

War and place names have more in common than geography. Across history, battlegrounds, factories and locales have lent their names to weapons and munitions—often linking them forever to conflict, ingenuity or the tragedies they wrought. Exploring these names constitutes not merely delving into trivia, but an absorbing journey through history, culture and the profound ways in which landscapes become part of the lexicon of warfare.

The 'Molotov cocktail' encapsulates how names can be welded from both propaganda and irony. It originated during the Winter War (1939–40) between the Soviet Union and Finland, when Finnish forces sarcastically dubbed the food parcels that Soviet Foreign Minister Vyacheslav Molotov claimed were being dropped over Finland as 'Molotov bread baskets'. In response, Finnish forces developed a bottle-based incendiary weapon—a crude yet effective makeshift device, more like a grenade—and called it the 'Molotov cocktail', a mocking retort to the Soviet claims of humanitarian aid. This weapon, if it can be called that, became extremely popular with guerilla forces the world over.[1]

---

1 Merridale, Catherine, *Red Fortress: History and Illusion in the Kremlin*, Penguin Books, 2013.

Stepping into early-era gunpowder-based arms, the 'Java arquebus' (or *Bedil Jawa*) from the Nusantara archipelago is named for Java. It denotes early long-barrelled firearms, akin to muskets, that were used before European contact. The term reflects both geographical origin and weapon type, tightly intertwined in name and identity.[2]

Some weapons reflect their origins through place names, even in subtle ways. The British 'Bren' gun is an early light machine gun whose name blends 'Brno', a Czech city where it was first manufactured, and 'Enfield' in England where production continued. Likewise, the 'Sten' submachine gun fuses the initials of its designers (Reginald Shepherd and Harold Turpin) with 'Enfield'. These are perfect examples of how location and people become etymologically tied to a weapon.[3]

A tube becomes a legend

In the annals of military innovation, however, few devices have had as enduring and global an impact as the Bangalore Torpedo. Conceived in the then quiet cantonment (cantt) town of Bangalore (now Bengaluru) in the early 20th century, this deceptively simple explosive device transformed the way armies breached enemy defences. From the muddy trenches of World War I to the fortified beaches of Normandy, and into the arsenals of modern militaries, the Bangalore Torpedo stands as a testament to ingenuity born of necessity. This tale traces its origin, evolution and legacy—both martial and cultural—through a century of warfare and remembrance.

---

2 Andaya, Leonard Y., *The World of Maluku: Eastern Indonesia in the Early Modern Period*, University of Hawaii Press, 1993.

3 Hogg, Ian V., *The Weapons that Changed the World*, Ebury Press, 1986.

The story begins in 1907 in Bangalore, then a British (and now Indian) cantt and home to the Madras Engineer Group (MEG), also known as the Madras Sappers. The MEG is the oldest Regiment of the Corps of Engineers of the Indian Army—drawing its origin from the erstwhile Madras Presidency army of the British Raj—followed by the Bengal and Bombay Sappers, from the Bengal and Bombay Presidencies, respectively, all three of which are in existence today. Nestled beside Ulsoor Lake, MEG was a crucible of military engineering excellence. It was here that Captain (later Lt Col.) R.L. McClintock, of the Royal Engineers, attached to the Madras Sappers, confronted a persistent tactical challenge, namely, how to clear barbed wire and minefields without exposing soldiers to enemy fire. McClintock's solution was both elegant and effective. He designed a device composed of metal tubes—each five feet long—threaded together and filled with explosives. These could be assembled into a longer pipe, pushed under enemy wire entanglements, and detonated remotely. The resulting explosion would clear a path wide enough for infantry to advance.

The first prototypes were assembled in just twenty-six hours, at a cost of nine rupees, five annas and ten paise, which, adjusting for various factors, would be about ₹2 lakh today.[4] In every way, a modest sum for a device that would revolutionize battlefield engineering! The first prototype was fired under Major (he had been promoted by then) McClintock's supervision by W.D.B. Conran, then a young officer serving under McClintock. Conran rose to the rank of Lieutenant Colonel in the Royal Engineers (Indian establishment) and was awarded the Distinguished Service Order. This initial design went through several

4 Dev, Arun, 'A torpedo named Bangalore', *The Times of India*, 29 June 2015, https://tinyurl.com/n4hecex2. Accessed on 10 November 2025.

improvements over 1911–12, making it more battle-worthy and capable of being assembled in the field.

Named after the city of its birth, the Bangalore Torpedo eventually made it to the world stage and into immortality. But why 'torpedo'? Because, in the military engineering of that era, the term 'torpedo' was not restricted to underwater self-propelled weapons but applied to any cylindrical object filled with explosives, which added another dimension to an otherwise simple device.

The Bangalore Torpedo saw its first combat use during World War I, possibly in April 1915 when the 20 and 21 Companies of the Madras Sappers took part in the Second Battle of Ypres. In the brutal trench warfare of the Western Front, it allowed the Sappers to clear obstacles while minimizing exposure to enemy fire—a critical advantage in a war defined by static lines and deadly no-man's-lands. Its true moment of prominence, however, came during World War II. Allied forces, particularly British and American units, adopted the Bangalore Torpedo for operations requiring rapid breach of fortified defences.

On 6 June 1944—D-Day—the device played a pivotal role. As Allied troops stormed the beaches of Normandy, Bangalore Torpedoes were used to blast through German barbed wire and minefields under intense fire. The US Army Rangers and British commandos relied on it to open paths for infantry and armour, contributing significantly to the success of the landings. The US military standardized the device as the M1A1 variant, packaging several five-foot sections in wooden crates. Each section weighed approximately 13 pounds, could be carried by one soldier, and contained a potent mix of TNT and amatol. This version was widely used in both the European and Pacific theatres.

Far from becoming obsolete after World War II, the Bangalore Torpedo evolved. It was deployed in the Korean War (1950–53), the Vietnam War (1954–75), the Yom Kippur War (1973), and numerous other conflicts. Its design was adapted to meet the changing demands of modern warfare, including urban combat and counter-insurgency operations. One notable advancement was the development of the Advanced Performance Bangalore Torpedo, which offered improved penetration and reliability. Another was the Bangalore Blade, an aluminium-bodied device that used explosively formed projectiles to slice through razor wire and other modern obstacles with greater precision and safety.[5] Today, variants of the Bangalore Torpedo remain in service with the armed forces of India, the US, Britain, China, Canada and Pakistan. Its continued relevance underscores the enduring utility of its original design, a rare feat in the rapidly evolving world of military technology.

The Bangalore Torpedo's legacy is preserved not only in military manuals but also in cultural memory. At the

5 'Bangalore Torpedo', *warhistory.org*, 13 December 2024, https://tinyurl.com/75rm6yaw. Accessed on 10 November 2025.

Madras Sappers Museum and Archives in Bengaluru, visitors can view faded photographs of Indian soldiers handling early prototypes, along with historical records and honours awarded to the Regiment. These artefacts serve as a tribute to the ingenuity and bravery of the Madras Sappers and their contribution to global military history. In 2016, marking the centennial of the torpedo's invention, the Madras Sappers introduced a commemorative cocktail named the 'Bangalore Torpedo'. This concoction—made with scotch, cardamom, jaggery, star anise, spiced apple juice, tea, and orange slices—symbolizes the fusion of Indian and British influences that birthed the device. It is now offered as a ceremonial drink to retiring officers, blending tradition with a touch of eccentricity.[6]

Beyond its tactical utility, the Bangalore Torpedo embodies a deeper symbolism. It represents the power of localized innovation—how a solution crafted in a quiet Indian cantt could ripple across continents and decades. It also highlights the often-overlooked contributions of colonial-era Indian military units to global warfare. The Madras Sappers, through their collaboration with McClintock, demonstrated that ingenuity knows no boundaries of rank or nationality. Moreover, the torpedo's enduring presence in military arsenals speaks to its adaptability. In an age of drones and cyber warfare, a century-old device made of metal tubes and explosives continues to serve. This juxtaposition of old and new reflects the layered nature of military history, where tradition and innovation coexist.

The Bangalore Torpedo is more than a weapon—it is a saga. A saga of necessity and invention, of colonial collaboration and

6 P., Suraksha, 'Bangalore Torpedo: Mine that defeated Nazis, and a malt', *The New Indian Express*, 18 January 2018, https://tinyurl.com/yckfn6yx. Accessed on 5 December 2025.

battlefield valour, of evolution and remembrance. From the trenches of World War I to the beaches of Normandy, from the archives of Bengaluru to the cocktail glasses of retiring officers, its legacy endures. In a world often defined by conflict, the Bangalore Torpedo reminds us that creativity can emerge from constraint, and that even the simplest ideas, when forged with purpose, can leave a mark far greater than their creators ever imagined.

7

Badge of Honour

Forging identity through formation signs

Standing on one of Meerut Cantonment's most frequented promenades, the Mall Road, is Ram House, the official residence of the Commander of 22 Infantry Division. At the gate, a polished brass plaque proudly declares 'RAM HOUSE', a name derived from the Division's emblem, commonly referred to as its formation sign: a charging ram mounted on a black background.

For devout Hindus unfamiliar with the military context, the name evokes Lord Ram, the most revered deity. Locals strolling past or walkers out for their morning or evening constitutionals pause, some bow and offer a namaste, while others place flowers. They treat it as a sacred shrine rather than a military residence. For serving soldiers, though, the sight presents a quietly amusing instance of reverence without intent. Yet, it is a testament to how entrenched religion is in our consciousness—and how emblems born of organizational need can take on an entirely different, devotional meaning when viewed from beyond, with a far-removed perspective.

But what's the view from within: the perspective of those who serve behind this symbol? For us, military symbolism is more than just ornamentation; it is a language in itself, of lineage, identity and *esprit de corps*. In the Indian Army, one such symbol, the formation sign, serves as a visual anchor of pride, purpose and recognition. Such insignia, worn as shoulder patches or painted on military equipment and even buildings, often unnoticed by civilians, is deeply embedded in the psyche of soldiers and formations alike. They are not merely patches on uniforms or flags, but living emblems that encapsulate history, myth, geography and aspiration.

What we believe in

Each formation, from Division upwards and even in the case of independent Brigades, carries a distinct visual identity. The background colour itself signals classification: a dark black for Infantry Divisions, and a bold red-white-red for Corps. Upon these backgrounds are embroidered emblems that range from animals charging into battle, to weapons raised in defence, or symbolic objects like keys, axes and swords. These signs are not chosen arbitrarily. Tradition dictates that the first commander responsible for raising a formation has the prerogative of selecting or even designing its insignia, a decision that often sets the tone for the formation's ethos and lore. This act of selection is both symbolic and strategic. It embeds the commander's vision in the DNA of the formation for posterity, creating a legacy that endures long after the individual has moved on. The emblem becomes a shorthand for the formation's character, its operational history and its internal culture.

Formation signs in the Indian Army are not without precedent. Their roots lie in British military tradition, where formation badges were introduced during World War I. Initially designed to mask unit identity while still distinguishing formations, these signs evolved during World War II to become widespread identifiers. They were drawn variously from geometric shapes, heritage, puns, or operational roles. The Indian Army inherited this tradition and adapted it to local contexts. Over decades, these signs acquired particular resonance. Unlike their British counterparts, Indian formation signs often draw from mythology, regional symbolism and linguistic nuance. They reflect not just operational roles but cultural identity as well.[1]

---

1 Roy, Kaushik, *War and Society in Colonial India* (1807-1945), Oxford University Press, 2012.

A most evocative example is that of 14 Infantry Division, affectionately known as the 'Golden Key' Division. Raised in June 1941 at Quetta during World War II, its insignia is a stylized golden-yellow key set against a black backdrop. The emblem is literal and metaphorical: a key that unlocks identity, recognition and pride. It reflects how early commanders embedded symbolism rooted in a geographic or experiential context. The Golden Key has since become more than a visual marker. It is a name, a reputation and a cultural artefact. Personnel from the Division refer to themselves as part of the 'Key', and the emblem finds its way into local references, from the headquarters' signage to informal nicknames for surrounding areas. In Dehradun, where the Division has been stationed for long, the term 'Golden Key' might refer to a building, a road, or even to the shopping centre that caters to military clientele.

On a lighter note, personnel of the Division often complain that '*hamari chabi lagi rehti hai*' (we are perennially 'keyed up')—a reference to their packed schedule and a pun on their formation sign.[2] The formation sign of 5 Mountain Division, located in northeastern India, features a red orb on a black background. It depicts the rising sun, but the red roundel has served to spawn the unflattering sobriquet of the 'a*se on fire' Division!

Another striking example is 2 Corps, raised on 7 October 1971 by Lieutenant General (Lt Gen.) T.N. Raina at Krishnanagar, West Bengal. It is widely known as the Kharga Corps because a silver *kharga* (scimitar) was presented to the formation on its raising by the Maharaja of Krishnanagar. (It is on display in the Officers' Mess at Ambala, where the Corps is now

---

2 Indian Army Archives, *Formation Signs and Regimental Identity*, Ministry of Defence, Government of India, 2015.

headquartered.) The Corps entered history through its decisive role in the 1971 Indo-Pakistan war, during which it achieved victories across Khulna, Jessore, Jhenida, Magura and Faridpur territories that now form part of Bangladesh. General Raina went on to become the Army Chief. General V.K. Singh was yet another Commander of 2 Corps who went on to become the Chief. I too had the good fortune to command this Strike Corps from December 2015 to January 2017. It is responsible for carrying out offensive operations in enemy territory, as it did in the 1971 war. There was no war during my tenure, though the Corps was involved in controlling, through peaceful means, the Jat reservation agitation which rocked Haryana in February 2016.

The Corps' emblem, the Kharga, which is associated with Goddess Kali, symbolizes divine destruction of ignorance as well as martial resolve. Its choice is telling, being evocative of mythological power, regional resonance and spiritual depth.[3] Superimposed on a red-white-red shield, the insignia marks it unmistakably as a Corps. Over time, the kharga became more than a symbol. It became the Corps' identity, lending its name to institutions, memorials and infrastructure.

The Kharga Corps is a reminder that Indian military symbolism often draws from indigenous traditions, blending martial history with cultural memory—as also in the case of the Bathinda-based 10 Corps. Its formation sign features Chetak, the horse of Maharana Pratap, combined with a human torso thrusting a spear—a symbolic nod to Rajput valour, mobility and readiness. Designed by its first General Officer Commanding Lt Gen. M.L. Tuli, it encapsulates agility and aggressive preparedness, boosting pride in rapid deployment

---

3 Chatterjee, Sabyasachi, *Cantonments and Colonial Urbanism in India*, Oxford University Press, 2019.

and decisive action.[4] Facing hostile terrain or demanding campaigns, a formation's emblem becomes a psychological anchor and a rallying point in adverse situations.

These emblems do not simply adorn uniforms or flags, they become very much part of daily language. 'Kharga' might refer to the Corps, the military exercise, the complex, or even the residence of the Corps Commander viz. Kharga House. 'Golden Key' might denote the Division's headquarters, its personnel, or the auditorium. Their presence extends from barracks to civilian areas, contributing to collective memory. In this way, formation signs become living emblems. They are chosen by commanders, imbued with personality and pride, and evolve into powerful names. They shape the formations and the places they inhabit.

Formation signs not only help forge identity, but also build up a healthy rivalry among formations. Soldiers identify with the symbol, seeing themselves as carrying forward its legacy. Whether it is the lethal precision of a dagger or the relentless prowling of a black cat, the emblem becomes a personal badge of honour. These signs often draw from historical narratives or spiritual symbolism, especially in formations raised post-Independence—rooting soldiers in a storied past and bestowing a sense of destiny.

Across the Army, similar shaping of identity occurs through emblem and speech, vividly illustrated by the Indian Defence Forum's compilation of formation signs. It is a treasure trove of nicknames, each reflecting character and locale. The 9 Infantry Division at Meerut is known as 'Pine', evoking resilience and rootedness, while the 12 RAPID (Reorganised Army Plains

---

4 Sawant, Prakash, *Symbols of Strength: Military Emblems and Identity in India*, Lokvangmay Gruha, 2010.

Infantry Division) is 'Golden Axe', a symbol of swift and decisive action.

These names stick. They morph into affectionate shorthand that seeps into everyday life within and around the formation. Soldiers refer to their units by these names, and civilians living near cantonments often adopt the terminology without knowing its origin. The emblems become part of the local lexicon, contributing to a shared memory that spans military and civilian spheres.[5]

Icons beyond olive green

The harmonious crossover and blending of military symbolism and civilian interpretation can sometimes—and often unintentionally, as in Meerut Cantonment—result in the meaning of the emblem splintering and turning the military command into divine realm. Extending beyond mere amusement, it shows how cultural symbols absorb layers of contextual meaning. A formation sign that symbolizes military might become, in civilian imagination, a spiritual icon. The dual interpretations—official and devout—coexist, often peacefully, even as one can delight in the irony. It is also emblematic of the quiet intersections where military culture meets public faith, each unaware of the other's roots. For visitors, it's a shrine; for soldiers, another quirk to chuckle about. It is a reminder that symbols, once unleashed, follow their own journeys, sometimes reverential, sometimes ironic, always weaving deep-rooted stories of identity and belief.

5 Indian Defence Forum, *Compilation of Indian Army Formation Signs*, IDF Publications, 2023.

Zooming out, there's a profound reality here: formation signs do more than distinguish military units. They encapsulate history, sanctify lineage and embody aspirations. The Golden Key is both literal and metaphorical, unlocking identity and recognition. The Kharga evokes power, myth and martial resolve. The Ram stands for strength, determination and, in civilian eyes, divinity. These emblems are not static. They evolve, adapt and imbibe meaning. They reflect the Army's ability to blend tradition with modernity, operational necessity with cultural resonance. They are visual poems—concise, evocative and deeply rooted in the Indian psyche.

And so, Army formation signs are more than insignia—they are a cultural map. They map the terrain of identity, belief and memory. Raised by commanders, they imbue personality and pride, and over time, transform into names, narratives and landmarks. They shape the formations and the places the latter inhabit. And sometimes, in moments of misinterpretation, they reveal how deeply religion, identity and symbol intertwine in the Indian consciousness. In the quiet, personal reverence outside Ram House, in the mythic power of the Kharga, in the unlocking promise of the Golden Key and in similar ramifications of many other emblems, we are offered a glimpse of the soul of military tradition. It is not just about who we fight for, but what we believe in.

8

Broad Arrow

This way up—or is it?

Military vehicles, with their distinctive olive-green colour, are not an uncommon sight on roads and public thoroughfares. But have you ever wondered why the vehicle registration number plates always have an upward pointing arrow? Some quip that it is to ensure dimwits know which side is up, and do not drive the vehicle upside down! However, practically, when equipment was airdropped in crates, a 'this side up' arrow did help in unpacking as well as in retrieving the items inside. The practice found its way into civvy street and now all packages, especially fragile ones, are marked thus.[1]

But the broad arrow symbol is a distinctive arrow pointing upwards used in combination with a number or additional markings and is a significant identifier in military and government contexts. As with everything else in the Army, this too has historical roots. It originated and was traditionally

1 Chatterjee, Sabyasachi, *Military Symbols and Their Evolution*, KW Publishers, 2018.

associated with the British military and Royal Army. It dates as far back as the 17th century, when it was first used by the British government to mark property belonging to the Crown during the reign of King James II (1685–88).[2] This was not restricted to the Army, but extended to the Royal Navy as well. During colonial times, the British used the broad arrow to mark specific trees in North America intended for shipbuilding, indicating they were reserved for the Royal Navy. There is also an instance from 1860 of the broad arrow being used in a salvage case, where a salvaged ship was marked with the symbol.[3]

The choice of an arrow as a sign was not a random one. It was historically a symbol of both direction and purpose, often used in military contexts to represent power, speed and focus. The arrow also connoted the idea of 'pointing in a specific direction', signifying the Crown's authority over all military matters, as well as the military's ultimate aim to defend the country. Over time, the use of the broad arrow became synonymous with government property, especially the Crown's ownership over military equipment. The upward-pointing arrow also symbolized a direction of authority or ascension and a connection to a higher power, such as the monarchy or state authority. The symbol is also associated with movement and progress, suggesting that these items or vehicles are part of a larger, organized system of state or military infrastructure (and not, as the wits suggest, an indication of which side is up). It was a clear and unmistakable symbol that said, 'This belongs to the king (or queen).'[4]

---

2 Knight, Charles, *The Broad Arrow: A Symbol of the Crown*, British Military Heritage Series, 2005.

3 Hewitt, Roger, *Naval Marks and Maritime Law in the British Empire*, Routledge, 2010.

4 Roy, Kaushik, *War, Culture and Society in Colonial India*, Routledge, 2011.

When first introduced, it was extensively used to mark all government property, including cannonballs. This not only signified that it was government property, but also served as an effective tool to prevent pilferage and misuse, which was quite rampant. The broad arrow acted as a deterrent. Anything with the broad arrow marked on it was considered the property of the Crown and could not be tampered with, misappropriated, or disposed of without official sanction. Instances of wagonloads of goods 'vanishing' were quite commonplace, but their disposal would become well-nigh impossible if engraved with the broad arrow. It was not restricted to bigger pieces of equipment; furniture, copper bolts in naval dockyards, and, in extreme cases, individual items of clothing issued to soldiers were also marked with it. This was vital, as officers, soldiers and sailors would sometimes try to smuggle goods or resell surplus equipment for personal gain.

The symbol, in fact, was so widely used that it earned a special place in military law. Needless to say, 'making away with government property' was, and remains, a grave offence, more serious than a theft of other property.[5]

As the British Empire expanded its influence around the globe, the use of the broad arrow symbol spread to various colonies, including India and most of the rest of the Commonwealth. With the establishment of British colonial rule in India, the broad arrow began to appear on Indian military equipment as well, which was standardized in line with British military practices. The broad arrow's adoption in India mirrored its function in Britain, marking military property as belonging to the Crown—and, after India gained independence in 1947, to the government. After

5 Prasad, Bisheshwar, *Military Law and Discipline in British India*, Ministry of Defence Archives, 1987.

Independence, the Indian Army retained many of the symbols and practices established during British rule, not only for the sake of continuity but also because they were already functional and deeply embedded in military culture.

Colonial past on wheels

India's adoption of the broad arrow was a result of both practicality and tradition; however, it is now restricted to the Armed Forces. Over time, the arrow became synonymous with the Army, and it was used on a variety of military equipment. Now it is restricted mainly to vehicles—of all types, including tanks and armoured personnel carriers.[6]

6 Mukherjee, Rudrangshu, *Symbols of Sovereignty: Colonial Legacies in Independent India*, Penguin India, 2016.

Army vehicles use a unique numbering system, distinct from civilian vehicles, that includes the broad arrow and a specific format to identify the vehicle and its class. This system helps in quick identification, especially in military contexts, and ensures vehicles are easily recognized by other personnel. This numbering system for Indian military vehicles is legally authorized and recognized in the same way as that for civilian vehicles but it is not restricted to any state or RTO, thus allowing for pan-India movement.[7] So the next time you are stuck behind an oversized army vehicle that is trundling along in the middle of the road and not giving way, the following guide will help pass time:

The broad arrow: It is the first symbol on the number plate, and signifies that the vehicle belongs to the Indian Armed Forces. In conversation, it is referred to as 'broad arrow' and abbreviated to BA No in written documents.

Year of commissioning/induction: The next two digits after the arrow represent the year the vehicle was commissioned into the military, not necessarily the manufacturing date.

Base code: The base code identifies the specific type of vehicle, often using letters.

- **A:** Two-wheel vehicles
- **B:** Cars and other general-purpose vehicles, like SUVs
- **C:** Light motor vehicles (1 or 2.5 tons)
- **D:** Lorry trucks (3 tons or more)
- **E:** Specialist trucks, cranes, etc.
- **P:** Buses, fire trucks
- **X:** Armoured vehicles (tanks and personnel carriers)

---

7 'Vehicle Registration Protocols for Armed Forces', MoD circular, Government of India, 2022.

Serial/vehicle number: The serial number is a unique identifier for the individual vehicle. These are typically six-digit numbers (maximum, but could be less), following the base code.

Check digit: The last letter on the number plate is the check code, used to verify correctness.

Despite the enduring legacy of the broad arrow in British military tradition, its use has waned over time. In the 21st century, the symbol is no longer as widespread as it once was not only in the UK but in most Commonwealth countries, primarily due to changes in both military and cultural landscapes. Modern British military equipment, including vehicles and gear, is often marked with barcodes, serial numbers and other identification marks that are more suited to digital tracking and modern logistics. The Australian Army still uses the broad arrow to mark defence-owned property. It is sometimes embellished with the letters 'DD' (Department of Defence) or 'WD' (War Department).[8]

In India, the broad arrow's use is now restricted to military vehicles. The arrow is a visual link to India's colonial past, a reminder of the country's historical military associations and its ongoing commitment to security—though, with the advent of technology and the passage of time, perhaps it is time to move on.

For now, if you see a vehicle with BA No ⬆ 94 **X** 1234C bearing down on you, it is better to get out of the way. Fast!

8 Australian War Memorial, *The Broad Arrow and Defence Property*, AWM Publications, 2021.

9

The Bent Nail

Those magnificent men in their flying machines

Of the three Services, the Air Force is perhaps the most glamorous, far removed from the muddy trenches that characterize land warfare or the seasickness that is an inevitable part of life at sea. This happy, couldn't-care-less attitude is best exemplified in the epic British comedy *Those Magnificent Men in their Flying Machines* (1965), which depicts an air race in 1910 and celebrates the daring spirit of early aviators, including real figures like pioneers Otto Lilienthal.[1] Little wonder because, after experimenting for over two centuries, the first manned heavier-than-air flight was the one by brothers Wilbur and Orville Wright in December 1903. The first flight, with Orville Wright at the controls, lasted 12 seconds, covered 120 feet and reached a speed of 6.8 mph (about the speed an average person can run). Altogether, they carried out three more flights that day, with Wilbur piloting the longest, covering 852 feet in 59 seconds.[2]

---

1 Baxter, John, *The Epic of Flight: The Age of the Pioneers,* Time Life Books, 1981.

2 Crouch, Tom D., *The Bishop's Boys: A Life of Wilbur and Orville Wright,* W.W. Norton, 1989.

Within two years of that, aeroplanes were flying for as much as 20 miles at a stretch. In 1909, barely four years later, Louis Blériot of France completed the first flight across the English Channel in his *Blériot XI* monoplane, demonstrating the aircraft's potential to cross borders. The same year, the first international air meet was held in Reims, France, where aviators competed for speed and distance prizes, igniting public fascination and laying the thematic foundation for the 1965 film.[3]

The two World Wars fuelled rapid development in the field of aviation including the formation of air forces as a separate service. Towards the end of World War II, the first operational fighter jet—the Messerschmitt Me 262—developed by Germany entered service in April 1944. It was followed by the Gloster Meteor, the first Allied operational jet, which entered service with the Royal Air Force on 27 July 1944, just one day after the Me 262's first combat victory. The most versatile, though, was the de Havilland Vampire, a pioneering British jet fighter aircraft. Its development started in 1941 but it entered service only in 1946, shortly after World War II—too late to see combat. Yet, it went on to play a crucial role in introducing many air forces worldwide to the jet age.[4]

In November 1948, India crossed a new threshold in its military aviation. The de Havilland Vampire jets arrived at Palam, ushering in the jet age for the Indian Air Force (IAF). It was the first Air Force in Asia to adopt a jet fighter. The pilots selected to fly these early Vampires were among the boldest and bravest—Squadron Leader C. Devaiah Subia (he was one of my father's heroes), Flight Lieutenant M. Patrick

---

3 Gibbs-Smith, Charles H., *Aviation: An Historical Survey from Its Origins to the End of World War II*, Her Majesty's Stationery Office, 1970.

4 Gunston, Bill, *Jet Fighters of the World*, Crescent Books, 1986.

'Micky' Blake, Flying Officers Verghese Kuriyan and George Douglas Clarke, and others. Flying these jets meant confronting unknowns: how to manage the new engines, how to cope with the stresses on the body, how to push speed and altitude in machines that were far more capable, and far more dangerous, than their earlier piston-engine predecessors.[5] One legend about those pioneering aviators (as recounted by later generations of IAF officers such as Air Marshal Philip Rajkumar) tells of how these Vampire pilots joked among themselves about the 'bent nail'.

Pilots are prone to telling tall tales and the higher they fly the taller the tale. The era of jet fighters brought in a new dimension in flying, that of extreme gravitational forces (G-forces). These G-forces subjected both man and machine to extreme stresses, physical and structural. For pilots, the G-force could be up to five to nine times the normal (1G is what one experiences momentarily in an ascending or descending elevator). This could be both positive and negative, making the blood flow towards or away from the brain—sometimes leading to blackouts with dire consequences. The early Vampire pilots would remark wryly that even a nail carried in the overalls became 'bent' as a result of these extreme G-forces. A good story to impress the ladies, no doubt, but still a myth! Later, anti-G suits were developed to counteract these G-forces, which is why modern-day pilots wear bulky-looking, padded flying suits. (They still manage to look dashing and debonair!)

---

5 Rajkumar, Philip, *The Vampire Years: Recollections of the IAF's Jet Pioneers*, Air HQ Archives, 2005.

That bent nail, of course, is metaphorical, an emblem of the extreme G-forces, the jolting pulls, rapid manoeuvres, loops, rolls, dives, and hair-raising moments that test the body's limits. It is a kind of fly-boy's charm because it marks the transition from the old to the new, from fragile wooden wings to roaring supersonic jets. It is in that pain, of pushing one's own thresholds, that heroism and self-belief are forged, much like Jonathan Livingston Seagull, the protagonist of Richard Bach's book of the same name.[6] A seagull who is trying to learn about flying, personal reflection, freedom and self-realization.

The bent nail embodies a wispy yet striking, utterly human, account from the realm of steel and speed, a flash of humour in the face of danger, an artefact fashioned by memory that reminded each pilot, and those who came after, of what it cost to tame the Vampire. That bent nail stands for endurance, the willingness to feel the body fight gravity, and the acceptance

6 Bach, Richard, *Jonathan Livingston Seagull*, Macmillan, 1970.

that wings bring not just exhilaration but stress as well. Proving oneself under extreme stress was part of what being a pilot meant then. And it continues to be so.

The Vampire was phased out of service in April 1975, though a vintage Vampire made a commemorative flight in 1989. The longevity award, though, goes to the Swiss Air Force, whose Vampires were the last to be retired from active service—in 1990. That is a testament to the design's durability and sturdiness.[7]

Maverick to Narry: What's in a call sign?

Alongside such symbolic references, air force culture across the world has long included vivid, living traditions of identity—namely, the custom of call signs. This practice of giving aviators shortened names or nicknames predates the IAF. In fact, much of the call sign tradition has been documented by Western air forces, particularly the US Air Force and the Royal Air Force, as well as the US Navy. It started with the advent of radio communication and developed substantially through World War II, the Vietnam War, and later conflicts.

Historians point out that nicknames were common among early pilots, but their advent as 'official' call signs, used over radio and in operational contexts/briefings, evolved later. According to the US Department of Defense documentation, call signs began to be informal identifiers among pilots, based often on physical or personality traits, memorable incidents or pop culture references. During World War II and afterward, as aerial combat operations, squadron communications, and ground control coordination intensified, call signs gained more

7 Watkins, David, *De Havilland Vampire: The Complete History*, Sutton Publishing Ltd, 1996.

importance, both for clarity in fast-paced operations and as part of unit identity.[8] However, the custom never caught on in the Army or Navy, except for some notable exceptions such as Lieutenant General K.J.S. 'Tiny' Dhillon (Retd). If at all, my nickname would probably have been 'Narry' and some of my course mates do call me that sometimes.

Popular films also reflect and amplify real-life traditions of call signs. *Top Gun* and its sequel *Top Gun: Maverick* are probably the most iconic, in which 'Maverick', 'Iceman', 'Goose' are used fictionally but mirror how actual call signs are often based on personality, physical trait, or a memorable incident. In *Top Gun*, Maverick is played by Tom Cruise, Iceman by Val Kilmer, and Goose by Anthony Edwards. Maverick, as the name suggests, is a cocky US Navy pilot, Iceman his talented but 'icy'-cool rival, and Goose is Maverick's wingman and best friend.[9]

Call signs also contribute significantly to the psychology of respect, seniority and comradeship prevailing in the Squadron. When a junior is addressed by his call sign by a senior or, conversely, a Squadron Commander by his call sign in formation, it reflects an informal structure of trust and cultural norms. These call signs transcend traditional and rigid hierarchical structures and become badges of belonging.

Many pilots say that sometimes they adopt their call signs so fully that being called by their birth name feels strange. Real-life examples from the IAF include Air Commodore Mehar Singh, affectionately called 'Mehar Baba', and Air Marshal V.K. Bhatia who was known as 'Jimmy', which has no connection to his

8 U.S. Department of Defense, *Call Sign Protocols and Tactical Communications*, DoD Publications, 2020.

9 Glassman, Julia, 'Let's Breakdown How All the Characters in 'Top Gun' Got Their Call Signs', *The Mary Sue*, https://tinyurl.com/5d4xntub. Accessed on 12 November 2025.

actual name. Air Chief Marshal R.K.S. Bhadauria, who was Chief of Air Staff and my contemporary, was known affectionately as 'Chhotu' on account of his short stature. But he happens to be one of the most large-hearted men I have ever known.[10]

So, Narry to Chhotu, over and out!

10 'Legends of the IAF: Mehar Baba, Jimmy, and Chhotu', *Bharat Rakshak*, 2021, https://tinyurl.com/y22xa2fj. Accessed on 12 November 2025.

SECTION III

WANDERLUST: MARCHING THROUGH HISTORY

10

Mhow or M.H.O.W.?

Where myth meets modernity

What connects the fine weave of Maheshwari silks and Chanderi cotton, the sheer comfort of handloom cotton bedsheets, and the divine taste of world-famous kulfi? At first glance, they seem to inhabit different worlds. Yet, they all belong to a town where military heritage is intertwined as finely as its fabrics and culture and is as sweet as its desserts.

Just about 20 km southwest of Indore, the largest and most populous city of Madhya Pradesh, lies Mhow, a relatively small town on the Malwa Plateau. Also known as Mau, it has a long and chequered history going back several centuries. In 2003, however, Mhow was renamed Dr Ambedkar Nagar after B.R. Ambedkar, the economist, jurist, social reformer and political leader, best known as the father of the Indian Constitution, who was born here.[1] His formerly humble home, which falls within the cantonment (cantt) limits, has now been converted into a grand memorial, attracting a large number of visitors, especially on occasions such as Ambedkar Jayanti (Bhim Jayanti) on 14 April every year.

The history of Mhow Cantt can be traced back to colonial

---

1 Chopra, P.N., *Ambedkar: Architect of the Indian Constitution*, National Book Trust, 2003.

times when the British established a garrison there in 1818, after the Battle of Mahidpur (1817), a decisive battle during the Third Anglo-Maratha war. The Holkars, who were defeated in this battle, had to relocate from their capital at Maheshwar, on the banks of the Narmada, to Indore. To keep an eye on the Holkars, who still remained a potent military force, the British thought it prudent to have a strong military presence nearby, and that is how the cantt at Mhow came into being.[2] Though it stakes claim to being the oldest cantt (as do many others), that honour goes to Barrackpore in West Bengal. It was established in 1765 for very much the same reasons (to keep an eye on the French) after the Battle of Plassey (1757).[3]

From about 1903, Mhow was the Headquarters (HQ) of the 5th Division, raised as a regular Infantry Division as part of Lord Herbert Kitchener's military reforms, and placed under British India's Southern Army, primarily for internal security duties. A few of its units, though, served overseas in World War I. In 1922, as part of post-war austerity measures, it was disbanded and its units absorbed elsewhere.[4]

A new 5th Indian Infantry Division was raised in Secunderabad in 1939, in the months leading up to World War II. It later acquired the unique distinction of having fought against all three Axis powers: the Germans, Italians and Japanese. Consequently, it earned a formidable reputation, and the nickname of 'Ball of Fire', taken from its formation sign, a

2 Gupta, Rakesh, *Cantonments of India: Colonial Legacies and Modern Realities*, Rupa Publications, 2011.

3 Roy, Kaushik, *Military Manpower, Armies and Warfare in South Asia*, Routledge, 2015.

4 Prasad, Bisheshwar, *Campaigns in World War I: Official History of the Indian Armed Forces*, Ministry of Defence, Government of India, 1987.

dark-red orb against a black background.[5] After World War II, unlike many other Divisions which were disbanded, it remained in suspended animation. It was resurrected in 1963 after the 1962 Sino-Indian war as part of the post-Independence Indian Army as the 5 Mountain Division, retaining its nickname of 'Ball of Fire' Division, responsible for the defence of Tawang (Arunachal Pradesh). The two Divisions thus had no shared history, but the commonality of the numeral '5' gives the impression of continuity.

Today, Mhow Cantt is home to three premier training institutions of the Indian Army, namely, the Infantry School, the Military College of Telecommunication Engineering (MCTE) and the Army War College.

The Infantry School, the oldest of the three, is also the oldest military training institution of the Army. It started as the School of Musketry in 1888 at Changla Gali (now in Pakistan), and was moved several times before its permanent relocation to Mhow in 1948. Brigadier (later Field Marshal) S.H.F.J. Manekshaw was the first Indian commandant of the School. All infantry officers cut their teeth at this School, starting from the Young Officers course. All senior infantry officers, including Army Chiefs, would have passed through its portals at least once.[6]

The MCTE started off as a simple School of Signals in 1911, before being officially designated as such on 1 October 1967. It is the alma mater of the Corps of Signals. Over the years, the MCTE has matured and now stands as a beacon of India's strategic communication and electronic warfare training,

---

5 Marston, Daniel, *The Indian Army and the End of the Raj*, Cambridge University Press, 2014.

6 Singh, Depinder, *Field Marshal Manekshaw: Soldiering with Dignity*, Natraj Publishers, 2013.

blending rigorous academic programmes with hands-on training and technological research. Through its collaborations with industry and academia, and focus on emerging defence technologies including 5G, artificial intelligence, quantum technology, electromagnetic spectrum operations and very large-scale integration, MCTE is at the forefront of shaping India's modern battlefield capabilities.[7]

The College of Combat was established in early 1971 within the precincts of, and as an adjunct to, the Infantry School by merging the Senior Officers' and Tactical Wings. It then became an independent entity and shifted (within Mhow) to its present location in 1988, and was rechristened the Army War College in 2003. The Army Training Command (ARTRAC) was also raised at Mhow in 1991, before moving to its current location at Shimla in 1994. The Army War College, Mhow, is in the vanguard of India's defence education, imparting tactical-level instruction and graduating to operational art, strategic foresight and technological collaboration. It equips officers from Major to Colonel rank with the ability to hold command and staff assignments in future battlefield environments, integrating doctrine, war-gaming and tri-service synergy. All officers of the Army, as well as a fair number from the Navy and Air Force, receive training in this top-tier institution.[8]

By virtue of three premier institutions being located here, almost every officer is required to come to Mhow at least once in his/her career. For infantry officers and those from the Corps of Signals, multiple tours to Mhow are a given, whether as students

---

7 Rao, S. Venkatesh, *Signals and Strategy: The Evolution of Military Communication in India*, Defence Research Press, 2019.

8 Chatterjee, Sabyasachi, *War Colleges and Strategic Thought in India*, KW Publishers, 2020.

or as faculty members. All officers have to mandatorily attend the Junior Command Course at the Army War College, so there is no skipping Mhow.

With so many training institutes, the strength of the military garrison is sizeable. Student officers and jawans coming to Mhow could be attending courses lasting from eight weeks to three years. This sizeable floating population is supported by a considerable permanent staff, who, along with their spouses and children, also add to the garrison strength. At any point of time, the garrison strength can be up to 40,000 to 45,000, inclusive of all ranks and dependants. Given the floating nature of the population, it is difficult to arrive at exact figures but suffice it to say that there would, at any point of time, be almost as many people living within the cantt as in Mhow municipality.

Consequently, the relation between Mhow Cantt and Mhow is symbiotic. The economy of Mhow is largely dependent on the cantt, and the garrison, in turn, cannot survive without the support of the locals for its daily needs.[9] The civilian town thus plays an integral role in supporting the cantt. The local businesses, which have been around for generations, cater to the military community—providing everything from tailored suits to military uniforms. Businesses like Moolchand & Sons (established in 1844 and the first of its kind) and R. Balchand (established in 1888) are reputed for outfitting officers in perfectly tailored blazers and suits. The *darzi* (tailor) would note down your measurements in an indexed ledger for use on subsequent occasions. You can bet that almost every Officers' Mess of the Army has at least one painting from Mhow, and every Army family has owned at least one dress or nightie stitched in the town's famous smocking style, not to forget leather shoes hand-made by wizened bootmakers bent over their cobbler's anvils. I still have a pair of brogues from there, remnants of my service days!

And who can ever forget the famous Mhow kulfi? Its USP, apart from its flavour, was the dilapidated Lambretta scooter from which it was sold. Even children learnt to recognize the sound of this particular scooter, weathered by time. Though nobody could ever decipher Sharmaji's street cry hawking his kulfi which would penetrate every house and even make pets' ears twitch in anticipation! Despite the passage of time, the quality of the kulfi remained impeccable. Meeting Sharmaji on subsequent visits to Mhow was like encountering a long-lost friend.

With their husbands busy studying, the ladies would have a ball, splurging on Maheshwari and Chanderi sarees, available at affordable prices. Even the shopkeepers knew how much an

9 Kumar, Ashok, *Military Towns and Civilian Economies: A Study of Cantonments in India*, Orient BlackSwan, 2016.

officer's pay was! The stationery shops did roaring business, thanks to the endless stream of assignments given to the student officers. They stocked and sold reams of bond paper, multi-coloured flashcards, OHP markers, pencils, sticky notes—you name it. Entering a stationery store was a sort of adult version of entering a toy shop.

The curious case of the backronym

With such a substantial Army presence, some witty people created a narrative that Mhow was actually the acronym for Military Headquarters of War (M.H.O.W.), during colonial times. However, while Mhow was indeed the HQ of the 5th Division, it was never the HQ of the Commander-in-Chief of the British Indian Army (this, during much of the war years, was at Shimla, the current HQ of ARTRAC). The institutions currently at Mhow are purely training institutions with little or no operational role. So, imagining Mhow as M.H.O.W. is pure fantasy. At best, M.H.O.W. is a backronym, an existing word or phrase converted into an acronym by those with fertile imaginations. A recent article in a national daily also refers to the cantt as '...Military Headquarters of War, near Indore...', further perpetuating this myth.[10]

In that sense, it is somewhat similar to SOS, the most notable example of a backronym. It became the standard distress signal for mariners in the era of Morse code, when three dots followed by three dashes and then by three dots (...---...), in a continuous stream, denoted SOS, something that was easy for a signaller

10 Das, Kalyan, 'Called 'fauji' at 3 by Prez Kalam, Harmanmeet becomes officer at 22, joins father's regiment', *The Times of India*, 14 December 2025, https://tinyurl.com/yndftkn5. Accessed on 18 December 2025.

to remember and transmit in an emergency. It is only later that people created the backronym of 'Save our Ship' or 'Save our Souls' when, in fact, the letters did not stand for anything. It was while enjoying the chapter on backronyms in Tharoor's *A Wonderland of Words* that the myth of MHOW as a prime military backronym immediately came to mind and that led to the idea for not only this chapter, but this book itself. Unlike Mhow, though, which has been renamed, SOS has survived through the ages and has now become the universal call for help, for any emergency in all walks of life.[11]

Mhow is a town of contrasts, a small seemingly quiet place, somewhat off the beaten path, little known outside military circles, though the Military Museum at Mhow, a first-of-its-kind museum and research centre in the country dedicated to the Infantry, is a must-visit for those interested in military history. Yet, its importance in India's military landscape is irrefutable. From its days as a colonial cantt to its current role as the heart of military training in India, Mhow is a town that continues to pulse with the pride, purpose and legacy of both its past and its future. And as long as the Army remains the cornerstone of Mhow's identity, the town's story will continue to unfold—rich in history, culture, customs and traditions, and a whole lot of spirit.

For Army officers, Mhow will always remain Mhow. In a sense, then, it is M.H.O.W. too.

---

11 Tharoor, Shashi, *A Wonderland of Words: Around the Word in 101 Essays*, Aleph Book Company, 2024.

11

Doolally

Worlds in a word

For a chosen few, it serves as an alma mater, where the thunder of artillery guns echoes alongside its enduring military tradition. For some, it is a heritage town, its sylvan surroundings imbued with the mythology, faith and culture of nearby sacred sites. For the rest, it stands among India's most historically resonant cantonments. Established during British rule, its legacy encompasses its role as a transit camp, its contribution to military training and logistics, and its linguistic heritage that persists in modern English slang.

Deolali (also spelt Devlali), situated in Nashik district of Maharashtra, lies approximately 200 km by rail to the north of Mumbai. It sits on a plateau about 550 m (1,800 feet) above sea level, surrounded by the Sahyadri ranges of Igatpuri and Trimbak, and bordered by the Dharna (or Darna) river.

The name Deolali or Devlali is thought to derive from the Marathi elements *deol* or *devla* (depending on the chosen spelling), meaning 'temples', and *ali*, the feminine expression for 'have come' or 'arrived', signifying perhaps a location where temples are prominent or first become visible (possibly while crossing the Sahyadri range). Local tradition suggests that pilgrims approaching Nashik, one of the four locations where the Kumbh Mela is held by rotation every twelve years, first saw temples from this area. Devotees from Pune and Ahmednagar (now Ahilyanagar) would halt for the night at Devlali, saying '*Devala Aali*', and then proceed to Nashik the following morning. Another version draws from *aali*, meaning a narrow street or path leading to the temple(s). It is quite similar in meaning to the English 'alley', though the two have no common roots. Over time, the spelling Devlali has gained currency, being easier to pronounce, though the official name continues to be Deolali—as reflected in government records.[1]

Historical accounts trace the Mughal rule over this region (Nashik) to as early as AD 1487. An important relic from this period is the Panch Batli Idgah in Deolali, believed to have been constructed by the governor of the Deccan, Khan Jahan Lodi, during the reign of Emperor Aurangzeb. From 1610 to 1700, control of Nashik changed hands between the Mughals and the Marathas, with the latter finally establishing authority in 1700.

A new chapter in Deolali's history began with the arrival of the British. To support their expanding military presence, a 'Staging Camp' was established here in 1861 to facilitate movement of troops by road from Pune to Mhow. In 1867, this was upgraded to a 'Rest Camp' where troops and families newly arrived in India could acclimatize, after disembarking at Bombay and before being moved inland to the Madras and Bengal Presidencies. It also served those who had completed their tenure in India and were waiting to be repatriated to Britain. The region was chosen in part for its milder climate, compared with the lowlands, which made it a location suitable for acclimatization as well as for rest and recuperation. Soldiers and their families who could not recover from illness were laid to rest at the Christian burial ground, which was constructed in 1868.

---

1 Citizen's Charter, Cantonment Board Deolali, 2020.

Deolali was established as a Class I cantonment (cantt) in 1869, and a Main Depot for arriving and departing British soldiers was formally opened in 1870.[2] These developments unfolded in tandem with the expansion of the Great Indian Peninsula Railway, which aimed to connect Bombay with other parts of India. As part of this endeavour, Devlali railway station came up in 1870. Two years later, the 'A' Officers' Mess (now known as the Heritage Mess) was constructed at a cost of a little over ₹30,000.

In 1904, the Army Staff College was raised here, although two years later it was moved to Quetta (now in Pakistan). After Partition, the Indian elements established a new Army Staff College at Wellington, in the Nilgiris, Tamil Nadu, in 1948. This was later renamed Defence Services Staff College in 1950 after incorporating the naval and air wings.

For the ordinary soldier stationed in the cantt, these rapid infrastructural and military advancements meant little. Troop ships sailed only seasonally (usually in the winter months) and so many soldiers were obliged to stay put for prolonged periods under conditions that were monotonous, physically trying, and mentally taxing, that too during the harsh summer months. Deolali's military garrison and hospital facilities, while providing basic amenities, could not alleviate the isolation, heat and boredom. European troops stationed here awaiting repatriation reportedly suffered breakdowns, malarial infections and other illnesses.

2 Roy, Kaushik, *Military Manpower, Armies and Warfare in South Asia*, Routledge, 2015.

These conditions contributed to the phrase 'doolally taap' (*taap* meaning 'fever' in Marathi), used in British Army slang to describe those exhibiting signs of mental strain. By the early 20th century, 'doolally taap' had been shortened simply to 'doolally', meaning mad, eccentric, or irrational.[3] The phrase entered military memoirs, medical records, letters and, later, popular culture. One contemporary British account refers to soldiers 'congregated prior to repatriation [...] some having mental strain after long station at remote or arduous postings, waiting at Deolali for sparse transport.'[4]

Deolali shot to prominence during World War I as a large body of British and Indian troops were stationed here before embarking for the European theatre. During this period, additional accommodation was constructed, and the cantt was expanded. As a result, after the War there was

3 Partridge, Eric, *A Dictionary of Slang and Unconventional English*, Routledge, 2002.

4 Martin N.A., 'The Madness at Deolali', *Journal of the Royal Army Medical Corps*, 2006.

surplus accommodation with piped water and electricity, suitable for housing new units. Around this time, 129 graves of Commonwealth Army soldiers from England, Australia and New Zealand were also consecrated, which still exist today—a solemn reminder of the human cost of conflict.

It was also during World War I that the term 'doolally' first appeared in official usage in the armed services. The cultural reach of the term has been magnified by its appearance in literature, popular dictionaries and even electronic media. The 1970s BBC sitcom *It Ain't Half Hot Mum* is set in Deolali, using the transit camp as a backdrop to portray and dramatize the colonial military experience. As if to support this aspect, Deolali is also home to several sanatoriums built by the Parsi and Gujarati communities, used historically and operational even today, for health, rest and recuperation.[5]

Yet, Deolali itself knew little respite. The cantt once again witnessed intense activity during World War II. It was referred to then as 'Overseas Rest Camp', since large numbers of units going overseas camped here. Alongside its function as a major transit facility, Deolali also housed a cellular jail, reflecting the British fondness for these particular establishments. A military prison with sixteen cells and intermediary detention recesses still exists. It is a matter of speculation whether it was built to move the chronic 'doolally' cases without exposing them to the general public, or to secretly move 'high-risk political prisoners' associated with the freedom struggle. What is known for certain, though, is that during World War II it housed prisoners of war of different nationalities from various theatres.

This period also marked Deolali's evolution into a centre for specialized military training. The Artillery School was originally

---

5 'Doolally', *Oxford English Dictionary*, Oxford University Press, 2023.

established at Quetta in April 1918 after World War I, and then moved to Kakul (both were part of undivided India, and are now in Pakistan) in April 1923. On 1 January 1941, the main body of the Artillery School relocated to Deolali on a single train pulled by two engines. It had been preceded by its advance party a few weeks earlier.[6] It was thereafter renamed the School of Artillery. After independence in 1947, British military assets at Deolali were transferred to the Indian Army. The transit camp role gradually declined, replaced by new military training, logistics and administrative institutions.

The School of Artillery remains one of the principal institutions in Deolali today, training officers and other ranks in field artillery, target acquisition and associated support roles. It conducts regular field firing exercises, the most important being 'Exercise Topchi', an annual firepower demonstration, on the co-located field firing ranges, an inescapable necessity for modern artillery training. These vast ranges offer the authentic military setting that filmmakers often seek: some of the shelling sequences in J.P. Dutta's war epic *LOC: Kargil* (2003) were shot in this dramatic locale, as were several scenes in Shyam Benegal's *Netaji Subhas Chandra Bose: The Forgotten Hero* (2004).

If you are curious to know how these cinematic details intersect with Deolali's evolution and that of the School of Artillery, you must visit the Rudranaad Centenary Museum. Inaugurated in October 2019 by President Ram Nath Kovind, as part of the centennial celebrations of the School of Artillery, it offers a fascinating record of this journey.

A short distance from Deolali lies Nasik Road, which is home to the Artillery Centre, which when combined with the School

---

6 Gulati, Y. B., and D.K. Palit, *History of the Regiment of Artillery, Indian Army*, Leo Cooper, 1972.

of Artillery makes the latter the largest such establishment in Asia. Adding further importance to this region is the Combat Army Aviation Training School, which trains helicopter pilots of the Army Aviation Corps.

With regard to the Indian Air Force (IAF), Deolali has over the years been home to a number of Equipment Depots (EDs). Records suggest that the first was 5 ED, raised in 1958 and disbanded/renamed to 25 ED in 1966. Then, 36 ED was formed in 1962, as an aircraft spare-parts depot, and redesignated as such in 1968. In 1983, 36 ED was merged with 25 ED. Over the years, these EDs played a vital role in managing a vast quantity of equipment and spares, mainly for aircraft of Russian origin—from the humble MiG-21 (phased out in September 2025) to the modern Su-30 and a whole range of transport aircraft. The EDs at Deolali thus serve as key nodes in the IAF's supply chain, ensuring spare parts and maintenance support for diverse aircraft fleets including the Aircraft Manufacturing Division of Hindustan Aeronautics Limited, Nashik, which is responsible for the licensed production of the Su-30.[7]

Truly, madly military

Now I come to my own connection to Deolali. My father, (late) Wing Commander M.S. Naravane (Retd), was posted here between 1959 and 1961, and it so happens that I was born in April 1960 at the Military Hospital in Deolali Cantt. (The hospital is a bit historic itself, having had humble beginnings as a Casualty Clearing Centre in 1871.) So, in a sense, my Army career began the day I was born! My father was posted in Deolali again over

7 '25 Equipment Depot', *Bharat Rakshak*, https://tinyurl.com/28ryv7d6. Accessed on 6 December 2025.

1974–76, just before I joined the National Defence Academy. I remember it as a hot, dusty and isolated place, far from the lively hustle-bustle of urban life. I can only imagine what it must have been like in the 1960s, let alone the 1860s!

Deolali is not defined by its military character alone. It is also home to the Barnes School (now known as Barnes School and Junior College), founded in 1925 by Archdeacon George Barnes, under the aegis of the Bombay Education Society. Notable alumni include Air Chief Marshal A.Y. Tipnis (Retd) and Admiral Karambir Singh (Retd), affectionately known as KB, who was the Chief of Naval Staff when I was the Army Chief, as well as a galaxy of film stars such as Dilip Kumar and Vinod Khanna, to name a couple. Interestingly, the Vinod Khanna-starrer *Imtihan* (1974) was filmed in the school.

Deolali/Devlali might be only a small town (the 2011 census pegs its population at around 54,000) but it illustrates brilliantly the complex interweaving of colonial history, military necessity, civic evolution and linguistic legacy. From its original establishment as a transit camp for British troops to its various transformations following Independence and its present role in Army training and Air Force logistical support, Deolali has retained its significance in India's defence infrastructure and in its contributions to civil society. Its geographic location offers strategic depth. Its elevation and distance from border regions make it suitable for logistical support, equipment storage, repair and refit, training and field firing exercises without undue risk. Equally, its position in English vocabulary as the origin of 'doolally' ensures that the memory of Deolali's colonial-era human experiences continues to inform language and culture. The cantt remains important not only for its operational functions but as a site of continuity of military culture, ceremonial traditions and identity. Ongoing attention to preservation of its heritage buildings, modernization of military facilities and balanced civilian-military fusion will determine how Deolali continues to serve both as a place of operational import and of historical resonance.

As for KB and myself, we are both doolally!

12

Daag-e-Shahi

Branding, punishment and haunting memories

From Wellington and Matheran to Mussoorie and Darjeeling, India's hill stations are ideal getaways to escape the heat and chaos of the cities. But behind this picture-postcard serenity of winding roads, verdant hillsides and quaint cafes, these landscapes reveal the unmistakable imprint of India's martial past. And of the many hill stations, Dagshai, in Solan district of Himachal Pradesh, offers a very distinct kind of military legend, rooted in colonial control, incarceration and spectral justice.

Few know that what is today a scenic and popular hill station seems to have had criminal antecedents. The name Dagshai is widely believed to be derived from 'Daag-e-Shahi', meaning 'royal stain', much like the *fleur-de-lis* used by the French to brand criminals and runaway slaves. Mughal-era criminals were allegedly branded with a hot-iron, possibly on the forehead, and exiled to this remote outpost—marking Dagshai as a penal settlement, a place of punishment. While this story is widely repeated in local lore and historical summaries, it remains uncited in official Mughal records, suggesting it may be part of a hybrid colonial-mythical narrative.[1]

1 Dhillon, O.P., *Dagshai: A Place of Royal Stain*, Allied Publishers, 1998.

Such tales hardly deterred British Army officer Robert Napier, who recognized the strategic value of this region during his survey in October 1846. He identified areas around the Solan Hills as an ideal site for new military outposts. To that end, the British East India Company secured five villages—Dagshai, Dabbi, Bughtiala, Chunawag and Jawag, in present-day Himachal Pradesh—from the Maharaja of Patiala. Remarkably, these were transferred for free, reflecting the cordial relations between Patiala state and the British at the time. The most prominent of the five villages lent its name to the cantonment (cantt), namely Dagshai. Perched in the Shivalik foothills, its elevation (5,689 feet/1,734 m) and proximity to the Kalka-Shimla Highway (then only a cart track) made it a defensible location. Besides, it had the salubrious climate so favoured by the British. Along with Sabathu and Kasauli, it formed part of a broader British strategy following the Anglo-Gorkha (Anglo-Nepalese) War of 1814–16 to quarter troops in cool and health-promoting hill stations.[2] As for Napier (who also oversaw the construction of Ambala Cantt), he served with distinction and ultimately rose to the rank of Field Marshal, holding the position of Commander-in-Chief in India in 1870.

Dagshai Cantt was established in 1847. In 1849, the 22nd Cheshire Regiment marched from Sindh to Dagshai, marking the beginning of its use as a permanent military station. Over the following decades, British Regiments rotated through the cantt. In a move redolent of past penal traditions, the British constructed the Dagshai Central Jail in 1849 at a cost of ₹72,873. It was a T-shaped, maximum-security prison with fifty-four cells, including sixteen solitary confinement units to imprison

---

2 Sethi, Anand, *Dagshai: A Cantonment in the Clouds*, Himachal Heritage Press, 2015.

rogue soldiers and political detainees. Designed to break the spirit, these cells were narrow, poorly ventilated and devoid of natural light. The infamous 'bread-and-water' punishment was administered here, with inmates forced to survive on minimal sustenance while confined in spaces barely large enough to stand.[3]

Dagshai's military significance grew during the 19th and early 20th centuries. It housed Gorkha mutineers following the First War of Independence of 1857, Indian detainees after the Komagata Maru incident in 1914, and, most famously, Irish soldiers of the Connaught Rangers who mutinied in 1920 against British atrocities in Ireland. Dagshai became the site of the last execution of a British soldier for mutiny when Private James Daly was shot dead by a firing squad on 2 November 1920.[4] His grave remained in Dagshai until 1970, when his remains were repatriated to Ireland, symbolizing a long-delayed reconciliation.

Dagshai also intersects with the Indian freedom struggle. Mahatma Gandhi spent a night in the jail voluntarily in 1920 to express solidarity with the Irish prisoners, underscoring the shared anti-colonial sentiment between Indian and Irish nationalists. In mid-2024, Ambassador of Ireland to India Kevin Kelly visited the jail and expressed the desire of the government of Ireland to erect an India-Ireland memorial within the precincts, as it was this rebellion which led to Irish independence.

---

3 Narayanan, Ananth, and Anand Sethi, *Dagshai Jail Museum: A Restoration Chronicle*, Army Heritage Series, 2012.

4 O'Connor, Fergus, *The Connaught Rangers Mutiny: Ireland and Empire*, Irish Military History Society, 2019.

In a grim twist of fate, Nathuram Godse, Gandhi's assassin, was later held at Dagshai in 1948, during his transfer to Shimla for trial. The jail thus became a crucible of ideological conflict, ironically housing both the apostle of peace and his killer.[5] A few years after Independence, the jail was abandoned and fell into disrepair, with Godse having the dubious distinction of being its last inmate.

Even as the jail slipped into disuse, various units and formations of the post-Independence Indian Army continued to be stationed at Dagshai from time to time and it is now permanently home to Army establishments affiliated to the Kasauli Brigade. In 2011, the then Brigade Commander, Brigadier [(Brig.), later Lieutenant General (Lt Gen.), now retired] Ananth Narayanan, and local historian Anand Sethi spearheaded a project for the restoration of the jail complex (which was being used as a dump yard for unserviceable stores of the Military Engineer Services) and converting it into a museum.

Today, the Dagshai Jail Museum preserves its colonial architecture, archival records and haunting ambience. Visitors can walk through the claustrophobic cells, view the original punishment registers and read letters from prisoners long gone.[6]

---

5 Gupta, Rajat, *Gandhi and the Irish Question: A Shared Struggle*, Penguin India, 2016.

6 Narayanan, Ananth, and Anand Sethi, *Dagshai Jail Museum: A Restoration Chronicle*, Army Heritage Series, 2012.

But Dagshai's legends are not confined to history books. The cantt is widely regarded as haunted. The cemetery, the jail museum, and Mary Weston's grave, locally known as the *Mem ki Qabr* (*Mem* being short for Memsahib and *qabr* meaning 'grave' in Arabic/Urdu), are focal points of ghostly folklore. Mary, an Army nurse and wife of Major (Maj.) George Weston, died in 1909 when eight months pregnant, and was buried in a marble tomb imported from England. Folklore holds that pregnant women who took marble chips from her grave would bear male children. Over time, the tomb was vandalized, and many claim to see Mary's ghost wandering near the grave, protecting it from further desecration. Visitors to the jail report cold drafts, whispered cries and fleeting shadows. Some speak of a woman in white drifting through the corridors, while others describe a feeling of being watched. The museum's silence is not empty but heavy with the weight of colonial oppression, personal tragedy and unresolved memory.[7]

In October 2025, my wife and I travelled to Kasauli to attend the Khushwant Singh Literature Festival, where I had the good fortune to meet Lt Gen. Ananth Narayanan, as well as Anand Sethi, who was very keen to show me around the museum—located about 14 km away. Unfortunately, that could not materialize. I also met author and historian Chandra Haas Bhasin, better known by his pen name of Raaja Bhasin, an old friend of mine from the days when I was posted at Shimla as the Army Commander, Army Training Command, in 2017–18. Bhasin was a bit sceptical about whether Mahatma Gandhi had spent a night at the Dagshai Jail, but these anomalies only add to the mystique surrounding this quaint hill station.

Incarceration to illumination

Today, Dagshai is better known for its Army Public School (APS)—established on 1 June 1986 by the then Chief of the Army Staff, General K. 'Sundarji' Sundararajan, and Lt Gen. R.S. Dayal under the aegis of Headquarters, Western Command. APS Dagshai has matured into a celebrated residential institution. The 40-acre residential campus is set within the serene military cantt, characterized by lush vegetation and commanding views of the surrounding hills. Existing British-era buildings, including a former Officers' Mess and regimental barracks, were thoughtfully conserved and reappropriated for school use.

---

7 Sethi, Anand, *Dagshai: A Cantonment in the Clouds*, Himachal Heritage Press, 2015.

At the same time, modern facilities were added to accommodate its functions as a residential, co-educational boarding school. This architectural fusion gives the campus its unique heritage charm and practical functionality.[8] The premises also harbour a rock edict referencing the Mughal-era legend of 'Daag-e-Shahi', embedded in the natural terrain of the school grounds, which serves to fuel further speculation about whether the legend is myth or reality.[9]

Over the decades, APS Dagshai has nurtured a remarkable group of alumni—aptly called Dapsians—who have made their mark in the military, arts, politics, industry and beyond. The list of military alumni who have distinguished themselves with their selfless service and acts of valour is hardly brief. It includes Brig. R.S. Cheema from the very first batch (1986) and Brig. Rahul Machhral, Sena Medal, from the 1992 batch, who are amongst the most senior serving officers. The (late) Maj. Udai Singh, Shaurya Chakra, Sena Medal, was also an alumnus; he laid down his life in November 2003 while fighting terrorists in Jammu and Kashmir. As General Officer Commanding, 2 Corps, and patron of APS, Dagshai, I had the honour of meeting his courageous parents at the school's Annual Day function in 2016. A bust of this brave officer on the school premises continues to inspire generations of students.[10] Other notable alumni include Vidyut Jammwal, the Bollywood action star who, as a proud Old Dapsian, visited the school to present his Filmfare award; Nikhil Naz, award-winning sports journalist and author; film actors Kulraj Randhawa and Rannvijay Singha and mountaineer

8 Narayanan, Ananth, and Anand Sethi, *Dagshai Jail Museum: A Restoration Chronicle*, Army Heritage Series, 2012.

9 Chopra, Preeti, *A Joint Enterprise: Indian Elites and the Making of British Bombay*, University of Minnesota Press, 2011.

10 APS Dagshai Archives, Annual Day Commemorative Booklet, 2016.

Rigzin Dolkar who scaled Everest in 2016.

From a penal settlement to a military garrison to a seat of learning, from Daag-e-Shahi to Dagshai, to Dagshai Cantt—this sleepy little township has seen it all over the course of almost two hundred years. At Dagshai, systems of branding, incarceration and ideological conflict gave rise to tales of haunting and spectral justice which linger even today. Officers posted here often speak of the 'Dagshai effect', a sense of disquiet that creeps in during solitary patrols or late-night inspections. Some Regiments have even incorporated local lore into their oral traditions, passing down stories of phantom sentries and ghostly prisoners as cautionary tales.[11]

Such off-beat locations remind us that military history is not merely a chronicle of battles and strategy. It is also a tapestry of human fragility, psychological endurance and stories told in hushed tones around flickering campfires. Whether it is through the human suffering of prisoners or the lingering grief of a colonial widow, each tale adds depth to our understanding of service, sacrifice and memory. In a nation where military heritage often focuses on valour and victory, Dagshai offers a counterpoint through stories of suffering, ambiguity and the unseen. These narrations encourage us to look beyond medals and monuments, to consider the emotional and spiritual toll of military life. And in doing so, these stations become more than places on a map; they become veritable mirrors of the human condition, framed by gravestones and stone walls, echoing with footsteps that may never have truly left.

11 Sethi, Anand, *Dagshai: A Cantonment in the Clouds*, Himachal Heritage Press, 2015.

13

Those Priceless Bazaars

Regulation, relaxation, rhythm

They are the lifeblood of India's bustling cities, where the pulse of commerce, culture and chaos intertwine so richly. Take a stroll through any, and you get a fair idea of the area's socio-economic and historical character. They also possess, most intriguingly, a distinct blend of military discipline and civilian waywardness which, when compared to the hugely different flavour of their counterparts in the metros, encapsulates a far more vivid historical picture.

These are the bazaars and marketplaces of small-town India that lie within or in the vicinity of cantonments. These bazaars, spread across the country and indeed the subcontinent, are not merely marketplaces; they are vibrant cultural hubs, repositories of history, and tangible symbols of the intersections between commerce, society and politics.[1]

Among them all, three markets that stand out for their historical significance as well as links to the military are Lal Kurti Bazaar, Sadar Bazaar and Rajman Bazaar. These bazaars, each with its distinct character, are inextricably linked with military garrisons in various ways, serving both as centres of trade and as witnesses to the ebb and flow of colonial and post-colonial history.

---

1 Chopra, Preeti, *A Joint Enterprise: Indian Elites and the Making of British Bombay*, University of Minnesota Press, 2011.

During colonial times, particularly after the Battle of Plassey in 1757, the British established 'cantonments' or military garrisons to house their forces across the country, but more so in North India. These cantonments were exclusively for military use and, for reasons of security, located some distance from the main township not only to maintain discipline among the troops but also to pre-empt local connections (or liaisons) that could undermine British authority.[2]

Danapur Cantonment (Cantt), reportedly established in 1765, is regarded as one of India's oldest cantonments. It was the only exclusively British cantt, whereas others housed both British and Indian troops of the East India Company. At one point of time, it was the largest cantt in Bengal. Another cantt in West Bengal, Barrackpore, is also among the oldest, established in 1765. It holds historical significance as the site where Mangal Pandey's revolt against the British triggered the First War of Independence in 1857, exactly a hundred years after the Battle of Plassey.[3]

These cantonments were, and are, well-ordered spaces compared to the hustle and bustle of the proximate civilian areas. It may not seem so now and would be even more difficult to imagine, but at the time of establishment they were really in the 'back of beyond'. Delhi Cantt, for example, which was established much later in 1914, was in a thickly forested area teeming with wildlife. Alas, all that remains today of that forest is 'The Ridge' with its ever-dwindling forest cover, protected only due to regular interventions by the Supreme Court.[4] In those

2 Roy, Kaushik, *War, Culture and Society in Early Modern South Asia*, 1740-1849, Routledge, 2011.

3 Mukherjee, Rudrangshu, *Awadh in Revolt, 1857-1858: A Study of Popular Resistance*, Permanent Black, 2001.

4 Chatterjee, Sabyasachi, *Cantonments and Colonial Urbanism in India*,

days, it would have taken a horseman the better part of the day to ride the 25-odd km from the Red Fort and its surrounding markets such as Chandni Chowk—one of the oldest markets in what is now Old Dehi—to the cantt.

Little wonder then that a number of smaller markets sprang up in the villages in the vicinity of these cantonments. They were vital in providing the garrison supplies for daily needs, from fresh vegetables and dairy products to other household essentials like cloth, upholstery and utensils. These local markets thrived on the custom given to them—both for official supplies and for knick-knacks bought by the troops for personal use.

In those days, the standard British uniform comprised thick red tunics worn with leggings or breeches. These local markets

Oxford University Press, 2019.

would thus be teeming with red-coated soldiers and over time they came to be known simply as Lal Kurti (red-shirted) bazaars.[5] I am pretty sure that if you live in or have visited any North Indian city like Ambala, Meerut, Kanpur or Ferozepur, chances are that you will be familiar with the local Lal Kurti Bazaar. You may have even shopped there, without realizing its deep historical roots linked to our colonial legacy.

Lal Kurti: History on its sleeve

The Lal Kurti Bazaar located in the cantonment town of Meerut is a bustling marketplace where you can find anything from army surplus gear to school uniforms for local children. The sheer variety of establishments, from musketry stores selling target paper and dummy cartridges to jewellery shops selling gold and diamonds, all jostling for space with mobile repair shops and hair-cutting saloons, makes Lal Kurti a miniature reflection of the mixing and mingling of military and civilian life in a shared space.

Lal Kurti is also a place where military history is preserved in its alleys. Meerut is historically significant for being one of the major flashpoints of the sepoy rebellion that led to the First War of Independence. The bazaar area, one of the crucial sites of resistance, stands as a reminder of the colonial past with its trappings of gunpowder and rebellion. Rebel soldiers, many of whom had initially served in the forces of the British East India Company, gathered in the bazaar to rally against their colonial masters. The commercial activities of the bazaar were temporarily disrupted as it became a centre of military unrest.

5 Prasad, Bisheshwar, *The Sepoy Mutiny and the Revolt of 1857*, Government of India Press, 1957.

The aftermath of the rebellion saw a significant transformation in the nature of military-civilian relations, and Lal Kurti Bazaar, along with other military marketplaces, had to adapt to the changing social and political landscape.[6] In Meerut itself, the cantt was spatially divided with the European lines in one part and the native lines in another. Such reorganization meant that the bazaar's paying clientele, supply networks and dependence on local vendors had to be tailored accordingly. The bazaars around cantonments were often economically and socially shaped by soldiers' needs (food, clothing, equipment), so any change in garrison force composition or deployment automatically had a ripple effect on the local economy.

However, this Lal Kurti is not to be confused with 'Lal Kurti' in relation to the 'Red Shirt Movement' or the 'Khudai Khidmatgar' (Servants of God). The latter, founded in 1929 and led by Khan Abdul Ghaffar Khan (popularly known as Bacha Khan or Frontier Gandhi) in the North-West Frontier Province of undivided India, adopted red shirts as a symbol of unity. These 'Red Shirts' or 'Surkh Posh' also represented sacrifice and freedom for supporters of the movement. Inspired by Mahatma Gandhi's principles, the movement was committed to non-violent resistance against British colonial rule and played a significant role in India's independence movement. The colour of their 'uniform' also signified their fight against colonialism and alignment with socialist principles.[7]

Standing in the marketplace can be moving. It is hard to forget that this was the place where the sepoys once mutinied

---

6 Deshpande, Meera, *Behind the Uniform: Personal Lives of Indian Soldiers*, Orient BlackSwan, 2019.

7 Misra, Maria, *Vishnu's Crowded Temple: India Since the Great Rebellion*, Yale University Press, 2007.

and now, generations later, you are watching the colour and spectacle of soldiers and their wives haggling over vegetables and civilians sizing up military-grade surplus stores on offer at bargain prices. In the here and now, Lal Kurti sheds its historical weight and becomes a reminder that the demarcation between military discipline and civilian life is never actually as rigid as might be imagined but more of a convergence of sophisticated military tact with street-smart skills.

Sadar sells its stories

Another market with military connections is the ubiquitous Sadar (meaning central or main) Bazaar, found in major cities and towns such as Delhi, Lucknow, Agra, Jhansi and many more. Sadar Bazaar in the heart of the cantt area of Delhi is perhaps one of the best examples of how army and civilian cultures coexist. The bazaar is a commercial powerhouse, drawing military personnel and civilians alike. However, unlike Lal Kurti, which leans heavily on military nostalgia, Sadar Bazaar is more modern and caters to a wider variety of needs, from consumer electronics to ready-made garments, spices, and everything in between.

Here, the diversity of the population-clientele is reflected in the variety of products as also in the humorous exchanges: '*Arre, bhaisaab* (Come, brother), buy this trinket for your wife. She will be pleased and who knows, you may get lucky tonight,' delivered with a rustic twang. Sadar Bazaar is where soldiers go to buy everything that might not be available in the in-house army canteen, from household goods to the latest Bollywood music CDs (yes, some things never change!). The civilian population also flock to the market for an assortment of goods, but what makes Sadar Bazaar interesting is the subtle interplay between the army personnel and the local vendors. The latter know which of their customers are military men by their demeanour and haircut, even if plain-clothed, and often charge them more than the locals. Here, a soldier's street-smartness is tested not by his superiors but by the vendors who know the art of haggling better than any drill *ustad* (instructor)![8]

In recent years, the role of Sadar Bazaar has shifted, though it continues to hold a special place in the cultural fabric of military towns. The mushrooming of shopping malls and modern retail outlets has influenced the shopping habits of military personnel, yet the historical significance of the bazaar as a military market remains. It still offers a quirky mix of old and new, where one can buy everything from an antique army helmet to a smartphone from vendors whose families have often passed down their businesses from generation to generation. Today, Sadar Bazaar continues to function as a commercial space, though more so for civilians than for military personnel.

Topkhana and Rajman: Haggling in the local lingo

A combination of *top* from the Turkish word for cannon or artillery and *khana* from the Persian word for house or place led to the creation of Topkhana Bazaars that sprang up in the vicinity of army garrisons. This compound word was adopted into Hindi and Urdu as *tōpkhānā* and subsequently into English in the mid-17th century. During the Mughal and British periods, topkhana referred to a building, depot or arsenal for manufacturing, repairing and storing artillery and ammunition. This is why many historic marketplaces and military areas across

8 Chatterjee, Sabyasachi, *Cantonments and Colonial Urbanism in India*, Mittal Publications, 2008.

the Indian subcontinent, like the Jahan Kosha Cannon site in Murshidabad and the Topkhana Gate in Patiala, bear this name, as do the adjoining marketplaces.[9] Some of the bigger cities may have all of these markets spread out in different parts of the cantt, depending on where the various Regiments were billeted.

Then, there are other markets with quirky names like Rajman Bazaar—the local adaptation of 'regimental', a word too complicated for them to pronounce—which represent a different kind of military-civilian interaction. Regimental refers to things related to a Regiment—a military unit composed of soldiers who share the same specialization or function. In cantonment towns, the word 'regimental' would often be used to refer to anything related to military Regiments, including markets, events or even areas where military personnel and their families gathered, e.g. a Regimental Parade or Regimental Dinner Night. Over time, especially in the casual, everyday usage of the local population, 'Regimental' became 'Rajman', sounding similar but evolving into a more informal, local term.[10] Located in places where the military garrison was less prominent, Rajman Bazaars are nevertheless still spaces where the military influence is palpable but not as overt as in a Lal Kurti or Sadar Bazaar.

One such Rajman Bazaar, located in the cantt area of Jalandhar, is the unsung hero of military bazaars. Unlike its more famous counterparts, Lal Kurti and Sadar, the Rajman Bazaar tends to be quieter and less touristy. It is the kind of place where locals go to shop for daily essentials, but it also carries that unique cantonment charm, a mix of regulation and

9 Roy, Kaushik, *War, Culture and Society in Early Modern South Asia, 1740-1849*, Routledge, 2011.

10 Prasad, Bisheshwar, *The Sepoy Mutiny and the Revolt of 1857*, Government of India Press, 1957.

relaxation that makes it an appealing choice for both soldiers and civilians.

Colonial policies of segregation, division and resource extraction resulted in a distinct urban social stratification around military establishments. Bazaars like Lal Kurti, Sadar and Rajman became key sites of this colonial process. However, they are now far more than just marketplaces; they form living proof of the complex and symbiotic relationship between military establishments, colonial legacies and local cultures. They stand as testaments to the intertwining of two very different worlds, of military discipline and of everyday hustle. Once, at Meerut, my wife and I were enjoying some *chaat* at a roadside *thela* when who should walk by but a few boys from my Battalion, quite amused to see their prim-and-proper Company Commander tucking into *gol-guppe* and *aloo-tikki*!

These markets serve as vibrant reminders that the military was, and remains, an integral part of urban life, shaping the goods sold, the people who traded, and the very ethos of the markets themselves. Today, they continue to thrive albeit in transformed ways, serving both as historical landmarks and as essential parts of the modern-day economy. Their continued existence underscores the long-lasting socio-economic impact of military garrisons on urban life, ensuring that the past remains interwoven with the contemporary in these lively, bustling markets. These bazaars serve to remind us that at the end of the day we are all one people: proud citizens of Bharat.

14

Dhai Murti

Sculpting the nation

Driving down Sardar Patel Marg towards Rashtrapati Bhavan, one arrives at its junction with Mother Teresa Crescent (earlier Willingdon Crescent). Located on the far side of the junction and impossible to miss is a set of eleven statues, colloquially known as Gyarah Murti. These eleven bronze figures depict the Dandi March of 1930, with Mahatma Gandhi striding purposefully forward and ten figures from varied castes, beliefs and livelihoods following behind. Together, they rally for a common cause and embody the spirit of unity in diversity. The sculpture was created by Devi Prasad Roy Choudhury in 1972 to commemorate the silver jubilee of India's Independence. Though widely believed to depict specific figures like Sarojini Naidu and Matangini Hazra, this is open to interpretation. The arrangement is largely symbolic, representing the collective voice of the common people united under Gandhi's quiet leadership.[1]

But the Gyarah Murti is not merely a tribute to the salt movement. It is a visual metaphor for the idea that resistance against injustice is not the preserve of a few, but the duty of the many. The figures are deliberately stylized, not hyper-realistic

1 Guha-Thakurta, Tapati, *Monuments, Objects, Histories: Institutions of Art in Colonial and Postcolonial India,* Permanent Black, 2004.

but evocative, suggesting that they represent not any particular person but the common citizen—the farmer, the student, the mother, and the elder. Their march is frozen in time, yet it has lessons for the present.[2]

Turning right at the junction gets one to another set of statues, the Teen Murti Memorial within a traffic island. Here, three dismounted cavalrymen, lances in hand, representing the Mysore, Jodhpur and Hyderabad horse Regiments, form a solemn tableau around a sandstone obelisk. Created by British sculptor Leonard Jennings in 1922, this memorial was inaugurated in 1924 on the 10th anniversary of the start of World War I. It honours the 15th Imperial Service Cavalry Brigade, whose Regiments executed one of the last cavalry charges of World War I, taking Israel's Port of Haifa on 23 September 1918. To this day, the Indian Army celebrates 23 September as Haifa Day. The inscription on the memorial reads, 'Their Name Liveth For Evermore'.[3]

It is from this memorial that Teen Murti Bhavan took its name. Built in 1930 as part of the new imperial capital of India—New Delhi—this palatial building served as the residence of the Commander-in-Chief of the British Indian Army. After Independence, it became the official residence of the first prime minister, Pandit Jawaharlal Nehru. He lived here for more than sixteen years until his death in 1964, after which the residence was converted into a museum by Indira Gandhi. Today, Teen Murti Bhavan houses various institutions including the Prime Ministers Museum and Library Society, and the Pradhanmantri

---

2 Chatterjee, Partha, *The Politics of the Governed: Reflections on Popular Politics in Most of the World*, Columbia University Press, 2004.

3 Roy, Kaushik, *Military Manpower, Armies and Warfare in South Asia*, Routledge, 2015.

Sangrahalaya, a tribute to every prime minister of India since Independence.[4]

The enigma of two and a half

Gyarah Murti and Teen Murti are quite straightforward in their representations. Eleven figures, hence Gyarah Murti. Similarly, three figures, so Teen Murti. But *Dhai Murti*? How can there be two-and-a-half statues? The name itself is a riddle. Can a statue ever be only half? Is it broken, unfinished or metaphorical? The answer lies in its composition.

Dhai Murti features two full figures: a soldier of the Assam Rifles—India's oldest and lone paramilitary force, raised in 1835—with *khukri* in hand and followed by a sari-clad lady. The third, smaller figure is of a child being carried on the shoulders of the soldier. The 'half' can also be interpreted as a reminder of the incomplete journey of peace, the fragility of legacy, and the intergenerational transmission of duty.

The story behind this composition emanates from the jungles of Northeast India, and relates to the darkest hours of the Burma campaign.[5] During World War II, the Japanese launched stunning attacks through inhospitable terrain and were able to subjugate most of Southeast Asia. After capturing Thailand, the Japanese forces surged further westwards. One arm of the offensive swung south through the jungles of Malaysia and captured Singapore by mid-February 1942. Another arm swung northwards towards Burma (now Myanmar) and the capital, Rangoon (now Yangon), was captured by early March 1942.

4 Pradhanmantri Sangrahalaya, https://tinyurl.com/7nf7kk94. Accessed on 21 November 2025.

5 Baij, Ramkinkar, *Collected Works and Commentary*, Lalit Kala Akademi, 1982.

Under relentless pressure from the Japanese, the British had no choice but to withdraw toward India. Along with the Army, thousands of civilians sought refuge in India with nothing more than the clothes on their backs. The Japanese juggernaut was invincible and was finally stopped more than two years later, in the famous Battles of Imphal and Kohima in June 1944.[6]

These refugees, fleeing the Japanese, had to face the most arduous ordeals, battling the thickest of jungles, incessant rains, wild animals and creepy-crawlies. It was in the face of this humanitarian tragedy that the Assam Rifles, specifically 2 Assam Rifles, came to the rescue. From March to September 1942, four platoons of this Battalion, Numbers 2, 4, 5, and 9, were the silent guardians of evacuation and refugee columns. Their responsibilities extended beyond the battlefield in securing escape routes, coordinating with local authorities and tribal chieftains, and supporting humanitarian activities. In part due to their efforts, a sizeable number of army troops were evacuated from Burma by 2 Assam Rifles.[7]

The most daring mission was the evacuation through Chaukan Pass, in present-day Arunachal Pradesh. In mountainous terrain with peaks reaching 10,000 feet and with the daunting Dapha river to boot, 2 Assam Rifles orchestrated a well-coordinated rearguard rescue action. Its soldiers faced varied threats, erratic Japanese movements, logistical constraints and the emotional strain of the refugees. The trials and tribulations at Chaukan Pass were relentless but 2 Assam Rifles, under the leadership of Captain (later Major) Geoffrey Abbott Exshaw Keene, were equal to the task. Fording twenty-three tributaries, battling rivers in spate and marching through

---

6 Allen, Louis, *Burma: The Longest War 1941-45*, J.M. Dent and Sons, 1984.
7 Latimer, Jon, *Burma: The Forgotten War*, Thistle Publishing, 2018.

unrelenting rain, they barely covered 10 to 12 km a day. Starved and exhausted, they persevered and made it back to India by mid-September 1942.[8]

The men of 2 Assam Rifles, a beacon of selflessness, had conducted a daring rescue and returned with Burmese evacuees. In extremely trying circumstances, Major Keene and his men had displayed magnificent courage and tenacity, earning the highest commendation. In the sepia hues of September 1942, a telegram delivered words of gratitude from the North Burma Government's administrator, Charles Frederick Byrde Pearce, to Lieutenant General Noel Irwin, the Commander of 4 Corps:

> For Gen. Irwin from Pearce. I saw Assam Rifles rescue party which returned to-day [Stop] They have done magnificent work in very trying circumstances and I am extremely grateful to them and to you for sending them [Stop] Glad to report men returned in good condition only two sick [Stop] Keene and men deserve highest commendation [Stop][9]

Not just commendation, the remarkable effort also drew heartfelt appreciation. As a token of gratitude, the Burmese government, tea planters and locals donated a sum of ₹4,000, probably in silver coins. From this emerged the stunning silver statuette of the Dhai Murti. Conceptualized by the reputed sculptor and artist Ramkinkar Baij, this masterpiece portrays an Assam Rifles soldier guiding a Burmese refugee woman and child to safety, symbolizing the Battalion's humanitarian efforts.

---

8 Palit, D.K., *Sentinels of the North-East: The Assam Rifles*, Palit & Palit, 1984.

9 Pearce, Administrator, North Burma, Telegram to Gen. Irwin, September 1942. Prasad, Bisheshwar, (eds.), *Official History of the Indian Armed Forces in the Second World War, 1939-45: The Retreat from Burma, 1941-42*. Combined Inter-Services Historical Section (India and Pakistan), 1952.

Two adults and a child—hence *dhai,* or two and a half—just as one would ask for tickets for a rail journey or to the cinema.

The trophy, notwithstanding its colourful moniker, is not merely a symbol of humanitarian effort; it is also an enduring source of inspiration for Assam Rifles in entirety. While 2 Assam Rifles continues to be the custodian of the original Dhai Murti, a larger, almost life-size, fibreglass replica finds pride of place at the Assam Rifles War Memorial at its headquarters in Laitkor,

Shillong.[10] It is also the official memento of the Assam Rifles, its black matte finish lending it a distinctive appearance, as well as a symbol of the force's motto, 'Friends of the Hill People'. As a souvenir, it is presented to visiting dignitaries as well as to officers on their being posted out. On completion of my tenure as Inspector General Assam Rifles (North) in March 2015, I too was presented with this keepsake, which finds place of pride in my collection.

Beyond its attractive silver facade, the Dhai Murti is a living testament to the 2 Assam Rifles' devoted service and stands as a symbol of hope, depicting the Battalion's commitment to aiding the families fleeing the invading Japanese. The resilience of the contributors, who had battled snipers, leeches, hunger, thirst and malaria, is embodied along with their gratitude in the sculpture.

The plaque on the trophy itself is deceptively simple, giving no hint of the saga of extraordinary human endurance and fortitude behind it:

PURCHASED OUT OF DONATIONS TO PERSONNEL OF THE 2ND BN. ASSAM RIFLES

BY THE GOVERNMENT OF BURMA,
THE INDIAN TEA ASSOCIATION AND OTHERS
IN RECOGNITION OF THE OUTSTANDING WORK
PERFORMED UNDER MOST
ADVERSE CONDITIONS BY ALL
RANKS OF THE BN. IN ASSISTING
REFUGEES DURING
THE BURMA EVACUATION
MARCH–SEP. 1942

---

10 Baruah, Sanjib, *Durable Disorder: Understanding the Politics of Northeast India*, Oxford University Press, 2005.

These three compositions, though frozen in stone, metal and other materials, are hardly inert: they exude inklings of motion with people moving forward, sometimes on foot, sometimes dismounted, sometimes on jungle paths. In unison, they remind us that history exists not only in the headlines of high government and politics but also in such gentle yet resolute figures that stand eternally in our cities, waiting for our gaze to bring to the fore those episodes again. The artistic choices behind these sculptures are themselves strategic. Leonard Jennings' imperial classicism, Devi Prasad Roy Choudhury's dynamic realism, and Ramkinkar Baij's representation of humanity all bring distinct visual languages to the table.

Dhai Murti, though less celebrated than the other two, is perhaps the most poignant. It captures the ethos of the soldier not as a warrior alone but as a guardian of humanity. The 'half' statue is a reminder that every soldier's story is part of a larger narrative which is unfinished, evolving and deeply human.

SECTION IV

NOT ALL HEROES WEAR CAPES

15

O Captain! My Captain!

(With due apologies to Walt Whitman)

Till death do us part

In one of his best-loved and most quoted poems, 'O Captain! My Captain!', Walt Whitman uses the metaphor of a ship and its Captain to mourn the assassination of President Abraham Lincoln. While this poignant elegy was first published in 1865, its central metaphor found its way onto celluloid with renewed relevance many decades later—first in Jean Negulesco's 1953 film *Titanic*, followed by James Cameron's blockbuster in 1997. Both films recount the tragic tale of the Royal Mail Ship (RMS) *Titanic*, the most modern ship built until then and considered unsinkable, which went down on its maiden voyage in April 1912. The Captain of the RMS *Titanic*, Captain Edward J. Smith, gained a kind of immortality for remaining on board and heroically going down with the ship as it sank after striking an iceberg.

This tradition (of a Captain going down with the ship) is older than the *Titanic* episode and can be traced back to naval lore, particularly among sailors who believed the Captain's duty to his ship was sacred. This idea has been immortalized in the *Titanic* story, and it was seen as the Captain's final act of devotion to duty, a demonstration of his ultimate responsibility—not only towards his ship but also to the sailors under his command. In reality, though, the 'go down with the ship' tradition is more of a myth than a practical reality.[1]

As a matter of fact, many Captains of doomed vessels did manage to escape and in some cases there were even accusations of dereliction of duty. A notable example is that of the SS *Jeddah*, a British-flagged, Singaporean-owned passenger steamship operating between Singapore, other British territories in Southeast Asia, and Jeddah. In 1880, it was transporting over 1,000 pilgrims from Singapore to Jeddah, the nearest port to Mecca in Saudi Arabia, as part of the annual Haj pilgrimage. A straightforward journey turned into disaster when the ship, already showing signs of wear and tear, encountered rough seas in the Indian Ocean. The *Jeddah* began to experience severe damage, springing some leaks in its weakened hull. Rather than staying aboard and managing the situation, Captain Joseph Clark, along with some of the officers, abandoned ship off Cape Guardafui, near the Horn of Africa, leaving the passengers and the rest of the crew behind. Rescued by another ship and taken to Aden, they reported falsely that the *Jeddah* had sunk. However, in a strange twist of fate, the ship's Chief First Officer

1 Lord, Walter, *A Night to Remember*, Henry Holt and Co., 1955.

had taken charge and managed to keep the ship afloat until it was eventually towed to safety to the port of Aden by a British ship. Interestingly, my own journey many years later passed through these same waters. In 1965, when my father was posted to France as the Assistant Air Attache, our family boarded the SS *Guglielmo Marconi*, an Italian passenger liner, at Bombay and our first port of call after casting off was Aden.

A court of inquiry found Captain Clark, who had fled the ship, guilty of gross misconduct and suspended his master's certificate for three years, effectively making him ineligible for command. The widely publicized incident and the scandal of a British Captain abandoning his passengers inspired Joseph Conrad to write his famous novel, *Lord Jim*. The fictional ship in the novel is named the SS *Patna*.[2]

Interestingly, this episode led to a deeper reflection on the responsibility of the Captain for maintaining discipline and moral leadership during crises. Abandonment of the passengers stood in sharp contrast to the growing ideal of a Captain 'going down with the ship', which became even more entrenched after the *Titanic* disaster of 1912. It also prompted the formalization of regulations and expectations regarding ship Captains; though nowhere does any of these imply that a Captain is duty-bound to go down with the ship, leaving it more in the realm of moral and ethical decision-making in times of crisis.

Nevertheless, this tradition is one of the most revered and sombre customs in naval history. The idea that a Captain should remain on board and meet the same fate as the ship and crew symbolizes ultimate devotion, above and beyond the call of duty. When disaster struck, whether during battle or due to a storm or any other calamity, the Captain was expected to take

---

2 Conrad, Joseph, *Lord Jim*, Penguin Classics, 2007.

responsibility for the failure of the mission. His sacrifice was seen as the final act of leadership, more of a symbolic ideal than a law or established naval practice for much of history.

Honour and sacrifice find anchor

The most prominent example of an Indian naval Captain going down with his ship post-Independence is that of Captain Mahendra Nath Mulla during the 1971 Indo-Pakistan War, aboard the Indian Naval Ship (INS) *Khukri*, a Khukri-class missile corvette which was deployed in the Arabian Sea as part of India's naval anti-submarine task force. On the night of 9 December, while conducting operations against the Pakistani Navy, INS *Khukri* was struck by torpedoes fired by the Pakistani submarine, PNS *Hangor*. Severely damaged, the ship soon began to sink. Captain Mulla was faced with a critical decision and gave orders to 'abandon ship'. He was last seen on the bridge, calmly smoking a cigarette, refusing to abandon his post. The ship sank with him still aboard. His final act was of ultimate sacrifice, embodying the traditional naval ethos of 'going down with the ship'.

Captain Mulla was posthumously awarded the Maha Vir Chakra, India's second-highest wartime gallantry award, for his bravery and leadership in the face of certain death. In total, eighteen officers and 176 sailors died when INS *Khukri* sank. However, many others were rescued, and the rescue operation was hailed as a success due to the efforts of Captain Mulla and his crew.[3]

The sinking of INS *Khukri* remains one of the most significant

---

3 Cardozo, Ian, *The Sinking of INS Khukri: Survivors' Stories*, Roli Books, 2006.

tragedies in the history of the Indian Navy, post-Independence. It serves as a potent reminder of the unwavering commitment to duty of naval officers, notable not only because of the tragic loss of life but equally because Captain Mulla's conduct became an example of the 'no man left behind' mindset that is central to the military ethos. In 1999, the Diu district administration constructed an INS *Khukri* memorial at Chakratirth beach. A visit to the museum, besides offering insights into naval operations, is a poignant reminder of the 'service before self' ethos.[4]

Captain Mulla's wife, Sudha Mulla, and daughters, Ameeta Mulla Wattal (then 14 years old) and Anjali Kaul (then 11), have kept his memory and legacy alive by contributing to many ex-servicemen-related welfare schemes. This story resonates deeply with me since I was then an 11-year-old myself, and would watch with a sense of trepidation when my father, who was in the Air Force, left for his duty officer stints at the Air Headquarters or for some forward air base.

Yet, Captains do not always have to go down with the ship—as reflected in the tragic sinking of INS *Andaman* (P 74), a Soviet-built patrol boat, on 21 August 1990. During an anti-submarine warfare exercise in the Bay of Bengal, the ship developed a leak in the stern steering area, which was a critical weakness. This led to flooding of vital compartments, including the engine room—that affected the ship's propulsion system. The vessel eventually lost power and began to sink in choppy seas. Commander Ashok Diwan, captaining the ship, oversaw the evacuation of the crew and ensured their rescue. His leadership during the crisis was recognized for the handling

---

4 'INS Khukri Memorial: A Symbol of Courage and Honour', incredibleindia.gov.in, https://tinyurl.com/3aa964zp. Accessed on 5 December 2025.

of the emergency, ensuring that sailors were evacuated as safely as possible. Fortunately, most of the crew managed to escape. Other ships that were part of the exercise responded quickly to the distress signal, and rescued Commander Diwan and many others from the water. However, fifteen sailors lost their lives in the disaster. The incident led to significant changes in operational safety standards within the Navy.[5]

These real-life incidents, with the Captain at the core, illustrate how credos can transform into reality, through traditions that evolve over time, particularly starting from the 19th and early 20th centuries. In the era of wooden sailing ships, when shipwrecks were not uncommon, Captains were not expected to sacrifice themselves in such dramatic or heroic manner. Chances of sailors being trapped below deck were minimal as wooden-hulled ships often broke apart and gunports offered escape routes. In fact, the Captain leaving an endangered ship was quite common in earlier centuries, with no stigma attached.

The notion of the Captain going down with the ship crystallized into a romanticized and heroic ideal, particularly after events like the *Titanic* disaster.[6] As naval leadership became more professional, the Captain was no longer seen as just a military officer but as a moral leader who embodied the values of honour, courage and sacrifice. Over time, naval traditions evolved, and the romanticized ideals of duty took hold, and Captains were increasingly expected to stay back—to show that someone in command would not shirk responsibility.[7]

---

5 'INS Andaman Incident Report', Indian Navy Archives, Ministry of Defence, Government of India, 1990.

6 Lord, Walter, *A Night to Remember*, Henry Holt and Co., 1955.

7 Till, Geoffrey, *Seapower: A Guide for the Twenty-First Century*, Routledge, 2009.

This deep sense of responsibility and duty is reinforced by the imagery in 'Casabianca', the famous poem by English poet Felicia Dorothea Hemans. Its opening lines exemplify the sentiments of heroism and duty.

The boy stood on the burning deck
Whence all but he had fled;
The flame that lit the battle's wreck
Shone round him o'er the dead.

The boy standing on the burning deck, the final act of staying aboard the burning ship, can be seen as a symbol of self-sacrifice and unshakable commitment to duty, even when death is inevitable.[8] The image of the boy on the deck, standing alone as the flames consume him, reflects a kind of virtuous heroism, of selfless duty that mirrors the symbolic tradition of the Captain's ultimate sacrifice. Though one is an actual person (the Captain) and the other a poetic symbol (the boy), both represent the same underlying idea that ultimate responsibility and loyalty are more important than survival, and that sometimes the greatest act of leadership is to stay until the very end. Whether through the dramatic lines of a poem or the real-life and often tragic heroism of a Captain, the tradition of going down with the ship reflects the moral burden of leadership. As also the intangible, irreplaceable bond between a ship, her Captain, and all those who sail aboard her.

---

8 Hemans, Felicia Dorothea, 'Casabianca', *Poems of Felicia Hemans,* William Blackwood and Sons, 1839.

16

Badluram

The man who never died

The parade state can be called possibly the most vexatious document in the Army. Starting from the Company level and going up the chain right till the Army Headquarters (HQ), it is compiled on a daily basis to arrive at the strength of the Army. The Company Havildar Major (CHM) of each Company of the Battalion, whose responsibility it is, sets the ball rolling. It usually follows a set format: Authorized Strength, Posted Strength, and then the outgoes (personnel on leave, hospitalized, at courses, etc.)—finally totting up the Present Strength of the day.

It is quite like a balance sheet, with the Posted Strength corresponding to 'assets' and the outgoes to 'liabilities', with the Present Strength being the 'cash in hand', the resources available for that day. The Authorized Strength and the Posted Strength rarely match due to a variety of reasons, like an overall shortfall in the intake or units in difficult field areas on the borders being given more personnel so that their Posted Strength will be more than the Authorized Strength, at the cost of units in peace stations—a vital management function.

The Company parade states are then compiled at the Battalion level by the Subedar Adjutant (SA), a Junior Commissioned Officer (JCO), who reports directly to the Adjutant of the unit, responsible for overseeing administration, training and discipline. This compilation rarely matches the figures held in the Adjutant's office—a few personnel will be extra or missing, a situation unacceptable by any accounting standards. The CHMs are then summoned by the SA for an audit. The reasons will usually be quite innocuous. For instance, a couple of jawans might have reported early in the morning and been 'Taken on Strength' by the HQ, but had not yet reached their parent Company and reported to the CHM. Or there might be a duplication—a Battalion team comprising personnel from all Companies concentrated in one Company for training purposes, but being shown on parade by all Companies. Once these anomalies are sorted out, the compilation is finalized, shown to the Commanding Officer (CO) and then forwarded to the Brigade HQ, the next higher formation.

At the Brigade HQ, the respective Battalion parade states are scrutinized to ensure that the Present Strength has not fallen below the mandated strength, which would differ for field and peace areas. It represents the minimum resources—the 'cash in hand'—to carry out the day's functions. It, therefore, falls on the CO to juggle the operational need of maintaining the minimum mandated strength against the competing administrative requirements of welfare, such as sending troops on leave at regular intervals. This exercise goes on all the way through the Division, Corps and Command levels, with each intervening HQ adding the strength of troops under its direct command, till it reaches the Army HQ by early evening—where by then it has acquired the more rarefied designation of Fighting Strength.

It is this Present Strength in its original, humble, no-frills avatar at the Company/Battalion level that is given to the Company Quartermaster (CQM) to cater to that day's meals—

breakfast, lunch and dinner, apart from mid-morning/afternoon tea and snacks (the latter usually a handful of *shakarparas* or a samosa). This figure becomes the ration strength of the day, on the basis of which rations are drawn from the store. Rations are issued in sufficient quantity for all the meals of the day based on scales for each item, from flour/rice to vegetables, potatoes (not counted as vegetables), sugar and so on. So, if the scale for flour is 600 gm per man per day, and the ration strength is 80 inclusive of all ranks, then the JCO QM (or JQM) would draw 48 kg of flour from the store and give it to the *langar* in-charge, who would make sure it lasted for the day's fare. This quantity would then be deducted from the stock in hand, with the JQM doing a quick check to see whether the balance stock would be enough for the rest of the month or there would be need for a supplementary demand for one or more items. If you are wondering why potatoes have a separate authorization and don't fall under vegetables, that is yet another story. But it does give rise to the common refrain that there are only two types of vegetables served in the Army: either *aloo-gobi* or *gobi-aloo*!

Rations for the month are drawn in advance from the Battalion store, which also maintains a reserve of about two months' supplies to cater for unforeseen eventualities such as enemy action or natural calamities like floods and landslides that may cut the unit off from supply chains. These reserves come in handy especially during such calamities when, 'in aid to civil authorities', a sizeable number of civilians also have to be fed. A peculiar facet of this arrangement is that if there is any balance in hand at the end of the month, it is carried forward to the next month and that quantity of rations will then be under-drawn. However, according to some undecipherable bureaucratic logic, in case rations are under-drawn in the first instance, that quantity lapses!

Company QMs are misers by default and hate going into loss. So, to cater for these eventualities and avoid being under-drawn, they tend to inflate their ration strength, building an 'unofficial reserve' or a buffer to cater for such eventualities. The latter might include some unexpected guests who might drop by, such as a neighbouring unit patrol party or stranded tourists or flood-affected refugees. In the QM vertical, these ration strengths are also totalled up the chain, including the 'extras' added by each of the QMs. Even if each CQM adds just one extra person, it becomes about five per Battalion and given that there are about a couple of thousand units or their equivalents, the total number of extras becomes a 'largish' number that could range from 10,000 to 20,000. This total ration strength also reaches the Army HQ in due course, usually as a monthly average for procurement and provisioning purposes. Rarely does the Fighting Strength match the 'feeding strength', the latter being far in excess—leading to heated debates as to which of the figures amounts to the 'truth'. This seems an odd point to be fighting over, but in it lies the story of our protagonist, Badluram, set against the Battles of Imphal and Kohima during World War II.

Misstep becomes a master stroke

The Battle of Kohima, fought from 4 April to 22 June 1944, on the hills surrounding Kohima in northeastern India, was one of the most fierce and decisive engagements of World War II. It figures among the top ten battles in the history of the British Army. Japanese Lieutenant General Kotoku Sato's 31st Division, approximately 15,000-strong, advanced through treacherous jungle terrain, encircled Kohima and established roadblocks on the road from Dimapur to Kohima and onward to Imphal. The British-Indian garrison, drawn mainly from the Queen's Own

Royal West Kent Regiment, the Assam Regiment and assorted units, numbering just around 1,500 inclusive of all ranks, was ordered to hold Kohima, overlooking this all-important lifeline.[1]

From 4 April, Japanese forces encircled the garrison, bombarding trenches and executing night assaults. The defenders were gradually pushed back toward Garrison Hill, where intense trench-to-trench confrontations erupted. The most ferocious hand-to-hand fighting took place around the Deputy Commissioner's bungalow, where only a tennis court separated the opposing forces. By mid-April, the isolated defenders were near collapse. The 2nd British Division was urgently deployed by rail and air, and reached Kohima on 18 April. It cleared the Japanese roadblock near Zubza on the Dimapur-Kohima road and succeeded in linking up with the besieged garrison. After stabilizing the situation, it continued onward and reclaimed lost ground. By 22 June, forces from Kohima and Imphal linked up at Milestone 109 on the Kohima-Imphal road, ending both sieges permanently.[2]

The British suffered around 4,064 casualties. Japanese losses were even higher: 5,764 dead in battle, with thousands more succumbing to starvation, disease and wounds. Along with the Battle of Imphal, the Battle of Kohima decisively halted the Japanese advance into India. It marked the beginning of the end for the Japanese, being their first major defeat in Southeast Asia. Military historians call it the 'Stalingrad of the East', and the British Army museum in London rates Kohima-Imphal as 'Britain's greatest battle'.[3]

---

1 Allen, Louis, *Burma: The Longest War 1941-45*, J.M. Dent and Sons, 1984.

2 Kirby, S. Woodburn, *The War Against Japan: Volume III – The Decisive Battles*, HMSO, 1961.

3 National Army Museum, Battles of Imphal and Kohima, https://tinyurl.com/aeytr7ws. Accessed on 5 December 2025.

The Kohima War Cemetery, built on Garrison Hill, is a serene yet powerfully moving memorial. The rows upon rows of Commonwealth graves, the Cremation Memorial, and the famous epitaph, *When you go home, tell them of us, and say, for your tomorrow, we gave our today,* make for a sombre experience, reminding us of the humanity behind the sacrifice.

The victory in the Battle of Kohima demonstrated that the Japanese momentum could be halted, shifting the strategic balance in the Southeast. It highlighted the effectiveness of air supply, jungle warfare tactics, cohesive multi-ethnic Allied forces and local tribal support. It remains not only a landmark in military history but a poignant story of endurance, courage and the forging of regional identity in Nagaland—a battle that deserves remembrance.

Out of this backdrop emerges the story of Badluram, a rifleman in the 1st Battalion of the Assam Regiment—one of the many who took part in this most famous of battles as part of the garrison deployed at Kohima. He was killed in the early stages of the clash, struck by gunfire. After his death, Badluram's CQM, either by accident or design, never removed his name from the ration strength. As long as the supply lines remained open, rations authorized for Badluram continued to arrive, accumulating into a small surplus. When the Japanese forces besieged the unit at Kohima and supply lines were cut, it was that extra ration stock that saved countless lives.[4]

4 Roy, Kaushik, *War and Society in Colonial India 1807-1945*, Oxford University Press, 2012.

In 1946, Major M.T. Proktor, moved by the saga of how the absurdity of drawing rations for a dead man long after he was gone eventually served to save lives, composed a marching song, '*Badluram ka Badan*'. Set to the tune of 'John Brown's Body / Battle Hymn of the Republic', its lyrics go:

> *Badluram ka badan zameen ke neeche hai*
> *toh humein uska ration milta hai*
> *Shabash, hallelujah...*
>
> (Badluram's body lies beneath the ground, and so we get his rations... Bravo! Hallelujah!)

'*Badluram ka Badan*' has become the regimental anthem of the Assam Regiment, sung at the Attestation Parade (*Kasam*

Parade) at their Regimental Centre in Happy Valley, Shillong, during passing-out ceremonies. The song is regularly performed on other occasions too, complete with marching, stomping, clapping and spirited footwork. It has even transcended borders. During Exercise *Yudh Abhyas* 2019 in the US, Indian and US Army troops sang it together, with the US soldiers spiritedly joining in the chorus: '...we draw his ration... Well done, Hallelujah.'[5]

Nothing embodies *esprit de corps* more than marching to celebratory lyrics about free food from beyond the grave! The tune and the story have remained staples at every Assam Regiment parade since, binding generations through shared history and cheeky pride. An instance of simple oversight (was it, actually?) became a life-saver in a perilous wartime scenario. Though emerging from danger and desperation, the story is celebrated with humour—making it all the more enduring and endearing. Fittingly, the song has journeyed from regimental legend to meme-sticker, TikTok audio track and viral Instagram reels shot on freezing mountainscapes in Sikkim. When someone asks why soldiers dance to a seemingly morbid song about a dead person's rations, the answer is simply that a small bookkeeping error turned tragedy into triumph.

Badluram never sought to be a legend. He didn't set out to be a hero, he just fought, died and got 'forgotten' by the QM in the proverbial fog of war. However, that simple omission, whether by accident or otherwise, made him immortal. His spirit saved lives, his name cheers recruits, and his tune unites soldiers even across oceans.

---

5 Drishya, 'Badluram Ka Badan: The History Behind The Assam Regiment's Iconic Company Song', *Homegrown India*, 15 November 2024, https://tinyurl.com/2a8j9wxw. Accessed on 25 November 2025.

So the next time you watch a military parade, listen carefully and if you hear *'Badluram ka badan zameen ke neeche hai...'*, you will know to pause with respect and understanding. You are momentarily becoming part of trooping in the footsteps of a legend whose legacy is not about any heroic deed in combat, but about something more mundane which nevertheless played a role in saving soldiers and winning one of history's greatest battles. And do join in in the chorus... Hallelujah!

17

Saintly Sentinels

Legacy in legend

In the high-altitude desolate calm of India's northeastern frontiers, where snow-capped peaks cradle stories of valour and sacrifice, two names are taken with reverence—Rifleman Jaswant Singh Rawat, Maha Vir Chakra (Posthumous), and Baba Harbhajan Singh. Though separated by time, circumstance, and the nature of death, both men have become immortal sentinels, guardians whose presence is palpable not just in folklore but also in the daily rituals of soldiers who believe that their spirits never truly left their posts. Theirs are not mere tales of heroism. They are living traditions, spiritual anchors and cultural touchstones that blur that tenuous frontier between myth and memory. Together, they form a tapestry of devotion that continues to inspire generations of Indians, both within and beyond the military.

As one crosses Se La Pass[1] (once a treacherous route made so much easier with the construction of an all-weather tunnel), there is a descent into the Nuranang bowl which slopes gently downward, culminating in Nuranang Falls. The route along the valley floor, bounded by grassy hills on either side and dotted with seasonal flowers, is indeed an idyllic stretch. And so it is known as a 'hidden monsoon paradise' with flowers blooming in

1 In Tibetan, the word *la* means 'pass'. However, since this may not be familiar to many readers, the term Se La Pass has been used.

abundance across the hillsides during the rainy season. Travelling northwards, the massif-like ranges that surround Tawang come into view. Before reaching it, the road descends through a series of hairpin bends to the Tawang Chu (river), then climbs again via Khirmu village into Tawang. The latter is an area of immense historical importance, as the sixth Dalai Lama was born here. Just before this descent starts, all Army convoys mandatorily stop at Jaswant Garh War Memorial. And so do most civilian vehicles, as Jaswant Garh is a much-touted tourist attraction.

A hero's vigil beyond death: Rifleman Jaswant Singh Rawat

Born in 1941 in the serene hills of Pauri Garhwal, Jaswant Singh Rawat was a jawan of the 4th Battalion of the Garhwal Rifles. He acquired legendary fame in November 1962 during the Sino-Indian War, in the fierce Battle of Nuranang in Arunachal Pradesh. As Chinese forces advanced with overwhelming numbers and firepower, Jaswant and his unit were tasked with defending a critical position, as the capture of those heights (it wasn't known as Jaswant Garh then) would have opened the route to Se La. Amid the chaos, Jaswant displayed extraordinary courage in charging and seizing, under heavy fire, a Chinese machine gun and then turning it on the advancing Chinese to devastating effect.[2]

When his unit was ordered to retreat, Jaswant chose to stay behind. With the help of two girls, siblings, of the local Monpa tribe, Sela and Nura, he orchestrated a remarkable defence. Some accounts suggest that he was involved with one of the sisters and

2 'Who was Jaswant Singh Rawat, the soldier who killed over 300 Chinese troops during 1962 India-China war?', *India Sentinels*, 19 August 2023, https://tinyurl.com/mr278nn3. Accessed on 26 November 2025.

didn't want to be parted from his beloved. Whatever the truth, it certainly adds a touch of romance to what would otherwise be a very terse military account. Over the next seventy-two hours, he held off the enemy by cleverly positioning weapons at multiple vantage points and, along with his loyal assistants, moving and firing from these multiple firing positions, creating the illusion of a full Company still in action. His tactics sowed confusion among the Chinese forces and delayed their advance, giving the Indian Army critical time to prepare defences at Se La itself. Unfortunately, Se La fell sooner than expected, not on account of any lack of valour by the men on the ground, but because of some panicked decisions taken at a higher level.

Accounts of Jaswant's final moments vary. Some suggest he was captured and executed; others believe he took his own life to avoid capture. The most plausible version, however, is that he was killed in action, fighting till the last bullet and last breath ('*akhri goli, akhri dum tak*'). It is also believed that when Sela learnt that he had been killed, she took her own life. Nura's fate remains unclear; some reports suggest she was captured, others that she jumped off a cliff to avoid capture, emulating Sela's choice. The rest belongs to layers of folklore and oral tradition, reflecting the mystique that surrounds such heroic tales. What is known is that the Chinese, in a rare gesture of respect, returned his severed head and a brass bust of the brave soldier to the Indian side after the war. Such an act speaks volumes about the impression Jaswant made even on his adversaries. In recognition of his valour, he was posthumously awarded the Maha Vir Chakra, and the Army established a memorial at the site of his last stand, naming it Jaswant Garh.

But what sets this tribute apart is not just the stone and plaque—it is the living ritual that surrounds it. Jaswant Singh Rawat is treated as if he were still on duty. Every day, soldiers make his bed, serve him tea at 0430h, breakfast at 0900h and dinner at 1900h, the same timings as followed by the rest of the outpost. His uniform is kept immaculate, his boots polished. On snowy mornings, they are sometimes found muddy, as if he had been out patrolling through the night. His name remains on the rolls, and he continues to receive promotions and symbolic salary payments. These acts are not mere ceremony—they are expressions of belief, of a bond that defies mortality.

In 2019, his story was dramatized in the film *72 Hours: Martyr Who Never Died*, bringing his legacy to a wider audience. Yet, for those who serve in the Garhwal Rifles and for civilians who visit Jaswant Garh, the film is only a shadow of the living legend. In fact, soldiers often remark in informal gatherings that Rawat is one of the Indian military's immortals, respected by both the Indian Army and the People's Liberation Army (PLA) of China.

I have visited Jaswant Garh many times and paid my respects to this valiant soldier. On such occasions, I would look around the mountains on each side and try to recreate his last stand in my mind. And I would wonder where I would deploy my forces, were I tasked with the defence of Jaswant Garh.

The stories of Sela and Nura, though, are steeped in both tragedy and reverence. Though historical records are sparse, their legacy lives on through oral tradition, military folklore and symbolic commemorations in Arunachal Pradesh. Sela Pass, Sela Tunnel and Sela Lake—all major landmarks in the state—are believed to have been named in honour of Sela. These are not just geographic markers but living memorials that commemorate her bravery and emotional bond with Jaswant Singh Rawat.

While Nura has no formal monument, her name continues to be spoken in reverent tones by locals and soldiers alike, though sometimes Jang Falls (also known as Nuranang Falls) at the very base of Jaswant Garh are referred to as Nura Falls. Her legacy survives more through oral storytelling and the shared memory of her role in one of India's most poignant military legends. Both women are seen as symbols of civilian courage, representing the deep ties between local communities and the Armed Forces in frontier regions. Their involvement in the battle dilutes the distinction between combatants and civilians, transforming them into spiritual figures in the folklore of the Northeast.[3]

Eternal guardian: Baba Harbhajan Singh

An even more intriguing story unfolds to the west in the border state of Sikkim. On the road from Nathu La to Jelep La, about midway between Sarathang town and Kupup village, at an elevation of 13,123 feet (about 4,000 m) above sea level, lies the memorial to Baba Harbhajan Singh. If Jaswant Singh Rawat is remembered for his battlefield brilliance, Baba Harbhajan Singh is revered for his spiritual presence.

Born in 1946 in Punjab, Harbhajan Singh joined the 23rd Battalion of the Punjab Regiment, and was posted to East Sikkim. In October 1968, while escorting a mule convoy near Nathu La, he tragically slipped into a nullah and drowned. His body was recovered days later, but the legend was only beginning. Soon after his death, a fellow soldier claimed that Harbhajan appeared in a dream, guiding him to the exact location of the body. This uncanny experience sparked a wave of belief that Harbhajan had not truly departed. Stories began to circulate of

---

3 'The Legend of Rifleman Jaswant Singh Rawat, Sela and Nura', ChaloHoppo, https://tinyurl.com/5de8ycmb. Accessed on 22 October 2025.

soldiers receiving warnings from him in dreams—alerts about impending attacks, terrain hazards and enemy movements. These predictions were often eerily accurate. In some instances, sentries about to doze off on dark wintry nights claimed to have been rudely slapped awake.[4]

A shrine (Old Baba Mandir) was built by the Army near Chhokya Chho, the site of the bunker where Sepoy Baba Harbhajan Singh was stationed during his final posting. It evolved into a site of pilgrimage over time. Reaching the shrine involved climbing about fifty steps which, in the rarefied atmosphere, made it difficult for tourists to access. Accordingly, a new shrine (New Baba Mandir) was constructed at the junction of the Kupup-Gnathang Road and the track toward Menmecho Lake, where all who pass make it a point to stop and seek the Baba's blessings.

This abiding faith has deep personal roots. I too sought Baba's blessings when I visited the original shrine on my first posting to Sikkim in 1980. I recollect Nathu La as a windswept pass where we would peer at our PLA counterparts through the loopholes of our bunkers, far removed from the tourist spot it has become today.

The main attraction of this site is the shrine itself where soldiers treat Baba Harbhajan as a living presence. His quarters are maintained with military precision: uniform ironed, boots polished, bed made. In the mornings, sheets are reportedly found crumpled, boots muddy—signs, perhaps, of nightly patrols. Harbhajan Singh was posthumously promoted through the ranks, eventually reaching the status of Honorary Captain.

4 Baba Harbajan Singh Memorial Temple, Tourism and Civil Aviation Department, Government of Sikkim, https://tinyurl.com/4n25ebd5. Accessed on 5 December 2025.

Until his symbolic retirement, he was granted annual leave, during which his belongings were ceremoniously transported to his hometown in Punjab. A seat was reserved for him on the train, accompanied by soldiers—a gesture that made ritual and reality almost inseparable.[5]

The Baba Harbhajan legend is made even more remarkable by its cross-border resonance. During flag meetings between Indian and Chinese troops at Nathu La, Chinese soldiers reportedly leave a chair vacant for him—a silent acknowledgement of his enduring presence. Such gestures reflect a shared respect that transcends politics and conflict. His shrine continues to draw visitors—soldiers, civilians and tourists alike—who come seeking blessings, protection or simply to pay homage to a man who, in death, became a guardian.[6]

5 'The two Harbhajans of Nathu La', *The Tribune*, 30 August 2023, https://tinyurl.com/5n8yz7tu. Accessed on 5 December 2025.

6 Sandhu, Kamaljit Kaur, 'Chinese PLA wary of Baba Harbhajan's spirit on Nathula Pass', *India Today*, 10 July 2017, https://tinyurl.com/mwv4az5d. Accessed on 5 December 2025.

Though Jaswant Singh Rawat and Baba Harbhajan Singh lived and died under vastly differing circumstances, their stories converge in profound ways. Both men are remembered not just for their service, but for the belief that they never truly stopped serving. Jaswant died in combat, his final stand a testament to tactical brilliance and unyielding courage. Harbhajan died in an accident, yet his spiritual legacy grew through dreams, rituals and reverence. Jaswant's memorial is a military post where he is still 'on parade'. Harbhajan's shrine is a temple where he is treated as a saintly protector.

Both are more than historical figures; they are embodiments of devotion, courage and the enduring spirit of service. Their stories challenge our understanding of death—rendering it not an end, but a transformation into legend. In Jaswant Garh, the thud of boots and the aroma of morning tea are evocative of a soldier still standing guard. In Nathu La, the quiet rustle of sheets and the gleam of polished boots suggest a saintly serviceman still watching over his comrades. These rituals are not relics, but living acts of remembrance, of belief, of respect and, most movingly, of trust.

In both cases, the Army has embraced their legends—not as superstition, but as expressions of faith, loyalty and cultural continuity. Their stories are woven into the daily lives of soldiers, shaping morale, identity and a hallowed sense of duty. These traditions also reflect a uniquely Indian synthesis of martial valour and spiritual belief. In a country where gods walk among mortals and ancestors are never truly gone, the idea of a soldier continuing his watch beyond death is not just poetic, but deeply resonant. Moreover, the reverence shown by Chinese soldiers in both cases embodies the universal language of respect. Even amid geopolitical tensions, these gestures remind us that honour and sacrifice are recognized across borders.

As India continues to evolve, facing new challenges and forging new paths, the legacy of these two men remains a steady flame. It reminds us that duty is not confined to life, that courage can echo across generations, and that sometimes, the greatest heroes are those who never truly leave. Their watch continues. And in that eternal vigil, we find not just inspiration, but a deeper understanding of what it means to serve, to believe, and to remember. A valuable lesson not only for those in the profession of arms, but for the world at large.

18

Pedongi

Four hooves, brave heart

'... [They] proved their worth during the Battle of Monte Cassino in 1944... Moroccan Goumiers...were able to transport gear...across the Italian mountains.'

'[...] the reality is [they are] the most efficient way to move supplies in really gnarly mountain terrain.'

'We are proud of these unsung heroes of Kargil.'[1]

And pray, who is all this fulsome praise for? Not for men or machines, but for fleet-footed, four-legged heroes. Again, not for dogs or horses. Here is the twist in the 'tail' (pun intended!). These tributes are for the unsung mules who have been silent, invaluable transporters of weaponry, ammunition, food and water, and the wounded in wars—no matter how difficult the terrain or weather.

Worldwide, mules have been a boon and a bane for armies, who have long had these wonderful but recalcitrant and stubborn

1 Allen, Louis, *Burma: The Longest War 1941-45*, J.M. Dent and Sons, 1984; Bimberg, Edward L., *Mountain Warriors: Moroccan Goums in WW II*, Stackpole Books, 2008; Ahmad, Mukhtar, 'Meet an unusual hero of the Kargil conflict: Mule 696', *Rediff.com*, 13 August 1999, https://tinyurl.com/yr2snxef. Accessed on 28 November 2025.

animals in their ranks. More sure-footed than horses and easier to maintain, intelligent enough and less skittish under fire, they have been around since Mesopotamian times, and continue to serve even in today's era of mechanization and high-tech. The Indian Army is no exception.[2]

Army transport is divided into two types, mechanical transport (MT)—comprising all types of passenger or load-carrying vehicles (cars, trucks)—and animal transport (AT), which includes horses but consists primarily of mules. The mules, in turn, are classified into two types, Mules (MA)—i.e. mountain artillery—and Mules (GS), i.e. general service.

MA mules are larger, standing about 14 hands tall, and can carry up to 100 kg of load in saddles designed to transport dismantled artillery guns, especially the 75/24 pack howitzer, which was in active service in the Army till quite recently. 'Hands' refers to the way the height of equines is measured—in terms of human hands from the ground to the withers (top of the shoulder). Originating from ancient systems, the hand unit was based on the breadth of a human palm including the outstretched thumb. Obviously, this measure would change depending upon the size of the palm, so it was standardized to four inches in England during the reign of Henry VIII (Horses Act, 1540). That system remains in vogue internationally.[3]

GS mules are smaller and carry loads of all types, from sacks of flour to ammunition boxes, of up to 80 kg. The 'load' could also be the ordinary rider or injured soldiers who are evacuated using a special saddle, the Hamilton saddle.

Each MA mule has a dedicated muleteer, while a pair of GS

2 Roy, Kaushik, *Military Manpower, Armies and Warfare in South Asia*, Routledge/Pickering & Chatto, 2013.

3 Thompson, E.P., *Customs in Common: Studies in Traditional Popular Culture*, The New Press, 1993.

mules shares one. The muleteers feed and water their charges and walk alongside, leading them, as part of AT convoys. The bond between the muleteers and their mules is no less than between mother and child.[4]

In the Army, mules were used extensively during all wars as well as for routine peacetime activities, mainly daily maintenance and for advance stocking of posts likely to get cut off due to adverse weather conditions, especially in snow-bound areas. During the summer months, mule trains ply up and down from the nearest roadhead, along narrow, treacherous trails, supplying the forward posts. The complete range of rations, including kerosene for heating and cooking, is stocked at each post for periods of four to six months. It is a nightmare of a logistical effort which keeps everyone busy throughout the summer months. Often, this movement has to be carried out in the hours of darkness if the area is under enemy observation or is likely to draw enemy small arms or artillery fire. It may seem like an ordinary administrative job but is in fact an extremely hazardous operational one. In such operations, during wartime and peace, many mules made memorable contributions which were recognized.

Trotting into glory

One such mule was Pedongi, who began her military career in 1962. Initially known only by her hoof-branded number, 15328, she served in the Indian Army Service Corps (ASC) as an MA mule. Mules usually remain nameless throughout their service, but Pedongi was exceptional. Over many years of extraordinary labour, she carried ammunition, food, medical supplies, and even evacuated the wounded across treacherous Himalayan

---

4 Roy, Kaushik, *Military Manpower, Armies and Warfare in South Asia*, Routledge/Pickering & Chatto, 2013.

terrain, often at heights above 17,000 feet. Her missions spanned decades. While most mules serve for about eighteen to twenty years, Pedongi served for thirty-seven years until she was retired in 1997. She breathed her last at Bareilly in 1998, a year into her 'retirement'.[5]

Pedongi became famous, though, not for these routine duties but for an act of heroism in war. During the 1971 Indo-Pakistan war, as part of an AT column in Jammu and Kashmir, she was captured by Pakistani forces. Subsequently, she was used by them to transport weapons, ammunition and stores in the forward areas. However, within two weeks, she managed to escape and walked nearly 20 km through battle-scarred landscape and treacherous minefields back to the Indian lines, carrying a medium machine gun and several boxes of ammunition that had been loaded on her.

Moved by her loyalty, the Divisional Commander directed the Commanding Officer (CO) of the AT Battalion to draft a citation. Pedongi was honoured with a bravery citation and a ceremonial blue velvet rug, which is almost akin to receiving the Vir Chakra, after which she was exempted from further load-bearing duties. This award was formally presented in 1992 at the 223 Corps Day function in New Delhi and she was officially named Pedongi, after the town of Pedong, an operational location in West Bengal, where she had spent many years early in service. Naming her was a break from tradition as mules were only known by their hoof numbers; Pedongi was the first mule to be so honoured, a trendsetter of sorts. She later entered the *Guinness Book of World Records* as the longest-serving military mule.[6]

---

5 Kumar, Ashok, *Animals in Uniform: The Role of Mules in the Indian Army*, Defence Research Press, 2002.

6 Guinness World Records, 'Longest-serving military mule', 25 March 1998,

In 2017, the ASC named their main lounge in the Central ASC Officers' Mess in Delhi Cantonment after Pedongi in tribute to her unparalleled service and legacy and to immortalize the AT units within Army culture. It represented the Army's appreciation of unsung heroes, two-legged or four-legged, and reminded officers of the legacy of fortitude and dedication in supporting mountain deployments. Beyond logistics, Pedongi became a symbol of loyalty and endurance. Soldiers often recounted how deeply they bonded with her during years of high-altitude patrols and supply runs, and the memory of 'walking behind mules for days' still resonates amongst many veterans.[7]

https://tinyurl.com/2h4jy8te. Accessed on 29 November 2025.

7 Pal, Sanchari, 'The Story of Pedongi, the Brave Mule That Won a Unique Award from the Indian Army', *The Better India*, 15 July 2017, https://tinyurl.com/mw8dcdww. Accessed on 6 December 2025.

Pedongi's fame stems from decades of unwavering service, courageous escape under enemy control, and symbolic honours—from a ceremonial rug to a lounge named in tribute. But her story is not unique; there are other mules that have displayed such exemplary traits, and have been decorated with medals and commendations, and enduring remembrance.

Hoof Number 122 was another model mule. Over several working seasons, he hauled more than 6,500 kg across a combined distance of approximately 750 km. This was at altitudes around 15,000 feet in the Tawang sector along the Line of Actual Control near China. For this extraordinary effort, he was awarded the Chief of Army Staff (COAS) Commendation Card in January 2023. Capable and calm, his 'steadfast physical presence and extremely composed temperament' was reputed to have a stabilizing effect on other animals and contributed to zero casualties in convoys.[8]

Going back in history, a mule known simply as the Grey Mule served with the Madras Engineer Group (MEG) of the British Indian Army. He worked in the North-West Frontier Province, Tibet, Iraq, Egypt and Palestine, operating under fire and amid harsh terrain, between 1891 and 1922. Most interestingly, he was part of the Younghusband expedition to Tibet in 1903. The mule became the MEG's mascot and, though strictly speaking not permissible under military regulations, appeared with campaign ribbons and even headed the Group's marchpast at the unit's 150th anniversary celebrations in 1930. He passed away in 1933, and was buried with full military honours in a quiet corner of the MEG and Centre at Bangalore. His hooves were made into inkstands that adorn the entrances to Monkey House (Centre

---

8 Indian Army, COAS Commendation Card Citation for Hoof No. 122, Army Headquarters, January 2023.

Headquarters), Officers' Mess, 4 Engineer Regiment and the Royal School of Military Engineering at Chatham, UK.[9]

Another famous mule was Jimson, the mascot of the 2nd Battalion, Middlesex Regiment. He carried ammunition in rugged terrain in British India and also during the Boer War (1899–1902) in South Africa. Although animals were not formally eligible for medals, he wore the India Medal (1895–1902) and the King's South Africa Medal (1901–02), and was taken back to England by his Regiment.[10] Mules were also indispensable in both the World Wars, particularly in Italy and Burma during World War II.

Yet, beyond their exceptional service, mules have their 'humour in uniform' moments too. Examples abound of *badmash* (naughty) mules who would trouble their handlers no end, but become most obedient and disciplined in the presence of officers. It was as if they had picked this up from observing similar behaviour in soldiers! And just like indisciplined soldiers, mules could also get 'marched up' to the CO to be penalized for various misdemeanours. The usual punishment for this was 'pack parade', with the guilty mule having to undergo extra parade bearing a heavier than usual load of bricks or sand. Sometimes one of the other mules in the section might give the offending one a sharp kick as if meting out their own form of justice. This has carried forward to the punishments given to jawans, who have to do '*pitthu* parade' if sentenced to undergo rigorous imprisonment in military custody.[11] As their distinct quirks and temperaments revealed themselves, muleteers also started

---

9 Bedi, Rahul, 'The Exceptional Career of the Madras Engineer Group's 'Grey Mule'', *The Wire*, 25 January 2025, https://tinyurl.com/nhpjmfv2. Accessed on 30 November 2025.

10 National Army Museum, 'Britain's Most Highly Decorated Mule', https://tinyurl.com/33r35rzy. Accessed on 29 November 2025.

11 Chakravorty, B., *Stories of the Indian Army*, KW Publishers, 2010.

giving affectionate names to mules, recognizing them as more than just inanimate hoof numbers.

From the harsh mountain trails of the Himalayas to the battlefields of Europe (there are contemporary reports of mules being used in the Ukraine-Russia war), mules have played a central logistical role during both war and peace. They transport vital supplies where vehicles cannot, sustain remote posts against extremes of weather and terrain, and bond with soldiers in ways that no machine can match. They exemplify strength, loyalty and resilience, as embodied by Pedongi and countless other unsung quadrupeds who, like soldiers, have stood firm where many others would falter.[12]

With the advent of modern technology, the era of military mules is possibly coming to an end. Prior to the Kargil War (1999), the Army was in the process of disbanding AT units. However, when terrain and heavy shelling made MT and helicopter use nearly impossible, mules became indispensable for supplying to remote, high-altitude posts and their service got a fresh lease of life.[13] Around 300 mules were pressed into service to carry arms, ammunition and other logistic loads to the mountain tops where the Army was engaged in fighting.[14]

Now, more than twenty-five years later, robotic mules and load-carrying drones, also referred to as mule-drones, are steadily making inroads into what was exclusively the domain of these quadrupeds. Though the load-carrying capacity of these mechanical mules is currently limited, there is no doubt that

---

12 Gupta, Suresh, *Unsung Heroes: Animals in War*, Roli Books, 2005.

13 Kumar, Ashok, *Animals in Uniform: The Role of Mules in the Indian Army*, Defence Research Press, 2002.

14 Ahmad, Mukhtar, 'Meet an unusual hero of the Kargil conflict: Mule 696', *Rediff.com*, 13 August 1999, https://tinyurl.com/yr2snxef. Accessed on 28 November 2025.

it will increase in future. During the Army Day Parade held at Pune in January 2025, the Army for the first time displayed its integrated robotic mules, also known as Multi-Utility Legged Equipment (MULE), as part of its operational capabilities. These robots are designed to enhance logistics, reconnaissance and security operations and will be particularly useful in challenging terrain and dangerous situations, offering a safer and more efficient alternative to their four-legged living counterparts.[15]

So, in one way or another, MULEs will always remain part of the Indian Army.

15 Defence Research and Development Organisation (DRDO), Army Day Parade Briefing: Pune 2025, Ministry of Defence, Government of India, 2025.

SECTION V

WHO SKILLS, WINS

19

Chak De Phatte

A tribute to the Khalsa

Sports form an important and inescapable part of the daily routine at the National Defence Academy (NDA), where discipline and a competitive spirit converge to inculcate both physical courage as well as mental robustness. Every cadet is expected to participate in at least one of the team games on offer—be it football, hockey or basketball—and being part of the squadron team is a matter of pride. All cadets are assigned to one of the many squadrons, numbered phonetically from A-Alpha Squadron through R-Romeo Squadron. Each squadron has cadets from all six terms—except Romeo, which is an all-girls squadron—that form part of the three-year course at the NDA. I was in Lima Squadron, part of the Third Battalion. At that time, there were only twelve squadrons, Lima being the last in line.

Towards the end of each term, inter-squadron competitions are held, the results of which count towards determining the 'Champion Squadron' for that term. The stakes are high as the honour of the squadron and that of their officer instructors are on the line. Needless to say, there is fierce rivalry on display, especially during the finals. These competitions are not just about physical skill but embody the essence of teamwork and camaraderie, which in itself is a battle-winning factor. Nothing symbolizes this better than the saying, 'The Battle of Waterloo was won on the playing fields of Eton', implying that the discipline, teamwork, character building and leadership qualities honed through sports and school life at institutions like Eton contributed to the British victory at Waterloo (1815). Eton College, one of Britain's most prestigious boarding schools, was founded in 1440 by King Henry VI, and is renowned for its rich history, considerable wealth and distinguished alumni, known as Old Etonians.[1] Notable military alumni range from Sir Arthur Wellesley, first Duke of Wellington and the renowned military commander who defeated Napoleon at the Battle of Waterloo, to General Sir Mark Carleton-Smith, Chief of the General Staff and my counterpart when I was the Chief of the Army Staff (COAS).[2] General P.P. Kumaramangalam, COAS during 1966–69, was also an alumnus of this institution.

One of the memorable facets of the sporting culture at the NDA relates to the vibrant and chaotic cheering parties, where every chant carries weight. During these matches, the extras (or those not involved elsewhere) form the 'cheering party'—the Academy's version of cheerleaders. Usually from the junior courses, they are a raggedy, sweaty lot, a far cry from the nimble and nubile, scantily-clad cheerleaders seen on TV during IPL matches. Their job is to support their team from the sidelines, bring on the refreshments during half-time and do sundry other activities. The most important, though, is to cheer for their teams with hoarse yells of encouragement to keep the momentum going, for players and spectators alike. The passion of the cheering party often makes the difference

1 Roberts, Andrew, *Waterloo: The Last Great Battle of the Napoleonic Wars*, HarperCollins, 2005.

2 'Notable Military Alumni', *Eton College Archives*, www.etoncollege.com, Eton College.

between a lacklustre performance and a winning one. The off-field competition among the rival cheering parties, as to who can shout the loudest, is no less intense than the rivalry on the field.

I have a vivid recollection of these goings-on. The self-appointed leader of the cheering party would herd all the first- and second-termers together and shout, 'UP! UP!' The others would respond with a vociferous 'LIMA SQUADRON!' or the name of whichever squadron they belonged to. When spirits flagged (not of the players, but of the cheering party), a well-aimed kick on the backside would infuse renewed vigour in the slacking cadet. The staid chant of 'UP! UP!' was soon replaced by the more colourful *'chak de phatte!'*, usually followed by *'nad de gilli!'* also, with the squadron's name hollered each time. So it would go 'chak de phatte—Lima squadron!' or 'nad de gilli—Lima Squadron!' Not knowing Punjabi, most of the cadets had little idea what these phrases meant (and I was one of them), but would nevertheless scream the squadron's name at the top of their voices, ever mindful of their posteriors. At the end of regulation time, the members of the cheering party would be as tired as the players!

But how and where did these expressions originate—phrases that have transcended generations, and become part of popular culture? Chak de phatte, literally meaning 'pick up the planks', is a phrase in widespread usage, made even more popular by the Bollywood film *Chak De! India* starring Shah Rukh Khan. Simply put, it is an exhortation to do well, to get up and move on, and generally to give one's best. It is particularly used in a sporting context to enthuse players with a sense of motivation and camaraderie. In some contexts, it could also mean 'to bring the house down'. No one really knows quite how this term originated or how it became part of popular Punjabi folklore, but it possibly has military roots, particularly in the context of Sikh military strategy.

Combat to celebration

During the 17th and 18th centuries, the Sikh Khalsa under Guru Gobind Singh and later Sikh leaders engaged in guerrilla warfare against the Mughal Empire. One of the tactics employed was hit-and-run raids on Mughal outposts, camps and convoys. These raids were swift, well-planned and executed with precision, often catching Mughal forces off-guard and leaving them scrambling to respond. One of the strategies during such raids was to target Mughal supply lines and communication routes, which often consisted of temporary wooden bridges constructed by them to cross rivers and other obstacles. The Sikhs, using their knowledge of the terrain and their ability to move quickly, would target these infrastructure elements to disrupt Mughal movements and resupply efforts.[3]

3 Singh, Khushwant, *A History of the Sikhs: Volume 1, 1469-1839*, Oxford University Press, 2004.

The phrase 'chak de phatte' likely originated in this very context of guerrilla warfare. After a successful raid, whether on a Mughal camp or a supply convoy, the Sikhs would often remove the wooden planks or decking from the temporary bridges to make them impassable. This tactic would slow down or even stop the movement of Mughal forces, especially during their pursuit of the raiders. Thus, after a successful raid, the Sikhs might have shouted 'chak de phatte!' or just 'chak de!', as a signal to dismantle these bridges, both a practical military tactic as well as a symbolic expression of victory. In essence, it was not just about dismantling bridges but also about sending a strong message of defiance and a symbolic warning—that the Sikh warriors would dismantle the very foundations of the Mughal Empire.[4]

The origin of the phrase 'nad (nab) de gilli' is even more intriguing. While the phrase 'chak de phatte' is relatively straightforward in its connection to the act of removing wooden boards from temporary bridges, 'nad de gilli' is more difficult to contextualize. This phrase might have its origin in the children's game of *gilli danda*, where a small tapered wooden peg *(gilli)* is hit as hard as possible with a wooden stick (*danda* or *nad*). In the context of the raids on Mughal camps, 'nad de gilli' can be interpreted as a phrase that symbolized the swift, forceful and disruptive nature of the Sikhs' military tactics. Just as the gilli in the traditional game is struck with precision, the Sikhs would strike with similar precision and speed in their raids, quickly incapacitating their targets and leaving the Mughals scrambling to respond.[5]

---

4 Fenech, Louis E., *Martyrdom in the Sikh Tradition: Playing the 'Game of Love'*, Oxford University Press, 2000.

5 Dhillon, Harpal, 'Tent-Pegging: The Forgotten Martial Art', *Sainik Samachar*, Ministry of Defence, 2019.

Another equally plausible explanation is that the 'gilli' refers to the wooden stakes or pegs used to secure the canvas tents during camping. 'Nad de gilli' would then mean the striking (uprooting) of these pegs from the ground by mounted riders, quite like the modern version of tent-pegging. This would leave the occupants floundering under the heavy canvas, unable to fight, and vulnerable to being then disposed of piecemeal. Both explanations convey the same underlying message—a call for swift, decisive and well-aimed action. Anyone who has seen riders in action displaying their tent-pegging skills will vouch for this. The sight of horses bearing down, hooves thundering, riders effortlessly balanced on their mounts with perfectly poised lances, plucking the peg out of the ground to the accompaniment of a vociferous war cry, is indeed awe-inspiring.

In the contemporary world, these phrases have evolved from their martial origins into symbols of resilience, joy and enthusiasm. But their historical roots in the struggles of the Sikhs against the Mughal Empire remind us of the power of words to galvanize people being persecuted for their faith. The aggressive, combative elements are no longer relevant and today they are used more in a social or sporting context. At the NDA, they are chanted with an enthusiasm that has to be experienced first-hand to be understood.[6] Whether in battle or in celebration, 'chak de phatte, nad de gilli' embodies the spirit of a culture that refuses to be vanquished and always finds a way to rise in the face of adversity. These calls are not just cheers but a reminder of the strength and determination that have motivated generations of soldiers, scholars and ordinary people who refused to give up in the face of injustice or hardship.

---

6 'Cadet Traditions and Squadron Culture', National Defence Academy Archives, NDA Publications, 2010.

So, the next time while doing the bhangra if someone encourages you with a 'chak de phatte!', let your martial spirit come to the fore, respond with a 'nad de gilli!' and dance with abandon. Whether you are breaking down barriers in the field or in life, remember to give it your all. And recollect the free-spirited, rhythm-driven chorus of the song '*Chak de phattey*' from the film *Khosla ka Ghosla*, which is all about embracing life's unpredictability, laughing at its absurdities and responding with wholehearted enthusiasm.[7]

Eh duniya utt patanga, kithe hath te kithe tangaa,
This world is like a kite—who knows where it'll go; sometimes in your hand, sometimes hanging from somewhere.

Rati kukdi dendi banga,
At night, the servile hen crows like a rooster,

E de chak de phatte.
Now go all out!

E duniya khel tamasha, e tedi medi bhasha,
This world is all spectacle and show, it speaks twisted, crooked tongues,

E thish bhish tha thoon shuhshan,
This is gibberish—fun, chaotic rhymes meant to mimic playful nonsense, keeping rhythm and tone,

E de chak de phatte
So go ahead—rock it! Bring the house down! *Chak de phatte!*

7 *Khosla Ka Ghosla*, directed by Dibakar Banerjee, music by Bapi-Tutul, UTV Motion Pictures, 2006.

20

Lezim and Malkhamb

Ethos of a people

In the rhythmic clang of cymbals and the synchronized stomping of feet, a traditional dance form pulses with the spirit of Maharashtra. But Lezim is far more than a mere folk dance, as often mistaken to be. It is a martial drill, a cultural emblem and a living testament to the physical discipline that once trained warriors and now energizes communities. Rooted in the *akhada*s of Maratha tradition and elevated by the legacy of Chhatrapati Shivaji Maharaj, it continues to bridge the past and present, blending combat readiness with communal celebration. It is widely performed during festivals like Ganesh Chaturthi and Holi, weddings, *jatra* (pilgrimage) processions, or even purely for entertainment as part of military tattoos and pageants.[1]

It also forms part of school fitness drills, as in my school Jnana Prabodhini Prashala, in Pune, where I performed in the school troupe on numerous occasions. In fact, our school troupe was very much in demand and lauded because of our discipline, punctuality and the precision of our movements. I remember that on occasions when the procession had to start in the early hours of the day, we would all sleep in the school

---

1 Gokhale, Shanta, *Folk Traditions of Maharashtra*, Sahitya Akademi, 2000.

itself to ensure we could assemble at the appointed time and place. We hardly ever slept, though, as we would be chatting throughout the night!

I don't recall what those conversations were about, but I am certain they never touched upon the cultural import of Lezim, the dance we performed, or the fact that its genesis lies not in the festive streets but in the austere training grounds of Maharashtra's akhadas—traditional gymnasiums where young men honed their bodies for battle. These dusty arenas were not just fitness centres but crucibles of martial ethos, where stamina, agility and coordination were cultivated through rigorous routines. Lezim emerged as a dynamic drill, combining rhythmic movement with strength-building exercises, where dance met discipline.[2]

Although its exact origins remain unclear, historical accounts suggest that Shivaji Maharaj, the architect of the Maratha Empire, revived and institutionalized Lezim in the 17th century as part of the military regimen. His soldiers, the *mavla*s, practised Lezim to build endurance and cohesion. The dance's formations, interchanging between rows, circles and concentric patterns, mirrored battlefield strategies, training warriors to move in unison, respond to cues and maintain spatial awareness under pressure, a codified combat drill. In Baroda (Vadodara), Gujarat, Lezim took on a military revivalist role during British rule, particularly when native martial practices were restricted. Incorporated into the school curriculum, these drills helped preserve indigenous combat traditions under the guise of physical education and culture.[3]

---

2 Deshpande, Sudhir, *Akhadas and Martial Culture in Western India*, Popular Prakashan, 1998.

3 Kulkarni, Uday, *Solstice at Panipat: 1761*, Mula-Mutha Publishers, 2011.

Among the three primary styles, military *lezim*, *talathekya* and *samanyajananna*, the military variant stands out for its martial precision. Popularized in Baroda and parts of Maharashtra, this form emphasized calisthenics, agility drills and weapon-less combat techniques. Dancers wielded heavier instruments like the *reedh* (bamboo pole) and *dhanusyasarakhi* (iron chain), turning the routine into a strength-training exercise. The choreography was not ornamental but served a tactical purpose. Step changes were signalled by a whistle, mimicking battlefield commands. Movements involved squats, lunges and jumps, echoing the demands of combat.[4]

Even today, the Maratha Light Infantry Regimental Centre at Belgaum (now Belagavi) incorporates Lezim into their ceremonial and physical training routines, preserving its martial essence, which is then carried forward to all the Battalions of the Regiment. No Raising Day or *barakhana* (feast) is complete without a performance of the Lezim or a Malkhamb demonstration.

While its roots are martial, Lezim has seamlessly transitioned into the cultural fabric of Maharashtra, as families pass down Lezim routines through generations, preserving not just steps but, equally, stories of valour, unity and resilience.[5] It is now a staple of Ganesh Chaturthi processions, village *jatra*s and physical training routines in schools. In towns like Sangli and Kolhapur, Lezim troupes lead processions with pride, often preferred over DJs or *dhol-tasha* groups on account of their traditional gravitas. This transformation from drill to dance did

---

4 Singh, Mahima, 'Lezim Dance–Ganapathi Dance of Maharashtra', *Auchitya*, https://tinyurl.com/bp7tc6vb. Accessed on 22 October 2025.

5 Patil, Ramesh, *Lezim: The Dance of Discipline*, Maharashtra State Cultural Board, 2007.

not dilute its discipline. Midnight *talims* (practice sessions) in local *mandals* still echo with the sound of cymbals and the bark of commands.

The Lezim instrument itself—a wooden idiophone fitted with jingling cymbals—is simple, cost-effective and functional. Variants range from lightweight sticks to weighted iron or bamboo poles used in strength drills, or even a length of cotton cord. Accompanied by drums like *dhol, dhalgi* and *halagi*, the music sets a tempo that dancers follow with military precision. Formations vary—twos, fours, circles and concentric rings—each demanding spatial awareness and timing. Regional styles like *Ghoti*, *Ghungroo*, *Dakhni* and *Palita* add flavour, reflecting local customs and musical preferences.[6] I also remember that one had to be careful not to let the folds of the loose kurta get between the cymbals as it left tiny cuts in the fabric.

Lezim is more than just a dance form; it is memory. It embodies the Maratha ethos of courage, coordination and community. Like *Povada*, which narrates Shivaji's exploits, or *Koli*, which celebrates coastal rhythms, Lezim conveys a symbolic narrative of martial pride. Its vigorous tempo and group formations evoke the spirit of collective strength, making it a living emblem of Maratha identity. Public showcases have amplified this symbolism, as when 400 performers demonstrated Lezim at the Delhi Asian Games in 1982.[7] Sangli's Guinness record in 2014—7,338 dancers performing in unison—is not just a feat of coordination but a declaration of cultural solidarity.[8] Lezim troupes from Maharashtra have graced

6 Sawant, Prakash, *Rhythms of Resistance: Music and Movement in Maharashtra*, Lokvangmay Gruha, 2010.

7 ANN News, 'The Marathas: The great fighters from central and coastal India!', https://tinyurl.com/ythyy84h. Accessed on 29 November 2025.

8 PTI, 'Sangli students set Guinness record for largest lezim dance', *Business Standard*, 26 January 2014, https://tinyurl.com/5f4bdhdp. Accessed on 29 November 2025.

Kartavya Path on Republic Day numerous times, reinforcing its place in India's cultural tapestry.

Apart from its military and cultural aspects, modern health experts recognize Lezim as a holistic fitness regimen. Its cardiovascular intensity rivals aerobic workouts, while its repetitive squats and jumps build lower-body strength. The dance steps enhance neuromotor coordination, balance and flexibility which are skills essential not just for dancers but also for soldiers and athletes alike. Psychologically, Lezim offers stress relief through rhythmic movement and group energy. Performing in troupes fosters confidence, camaraderie and social bonding. For adolescents, especially girls, Lezim has proven to boost self-esteem and reduce stage fright, while reinforcing cultural connection and pride.[9]

Lezim's survival owes much to grassroots and institutional efforts. Schools, mandals and community associations conduct structured classes, with separate troupes for children, women and seniors. Military and paramilitary units uphold Lezim as part of their physical regimen, reinforcing its martial lineage. Media and academia have also played a role. Lezim features in competitive exams, cultural documentaries and films like *Chhaava*, which dramatize its historical significance. These platforms ensure that Lezim is not relegated to nostalgia but remains a vibrant, evolving tradition.

---

9 Joshi, Meenal, 'Traditional Fitness and Adolescent Health in Maharashtra', *Indian Journal of Physical Education*, Vol. 12, No. 2, 2021, pp. 130–140.

Maharashtra's martial DNA

Malkhamb, Lezim's cousin, so to say, and also closely associated with Maharashtra, is often described as India's vertical gymnastics. However, it is far more than a sport; it is a martial discipline, a cultural artefact and a symbol of indigenous physical training. Derived from the Sanskrit words *malla* (wrestler) and *khamb* (pole), Malkhamb translates to 'wrestler's pole', reflecting its original purpose as a training tool for warriors. From its ancient roots in the akhadas of Maharashtra to its contemporary presence in national and international arenas, Malkhamb embodies the fusion of strength, agility and spiritual focus.[10]

10 Gokhale, Shanta, *Folk Traditions of Maharashtra*, Sahitya Akademi, 2000.

The earliest reference to Malkhamb appears in the *Manasollasa* (1135 CE), authored by King Someshvara III of the Western Chalukya dynasty, which describes wrestlers performing exercises on poles to enhance agility and strength. Archaeological evidence drawn from Chandraketugarh pottery (2nd century BCE) and Rajput paintings (1610 CE) depict pole-based acrobatics, suggesting a long-standing tradition of vertical training in Indian martial culture.[11]

However, the sport's modern revival is credited to Balambhatta Dada Deodhar, the physical training instructor to Peshwa Bajirao II in the early 19th century. In recognition of its utility in guerrilla warfare, especially for unarmed combat, Malkhamb was used to train soldiers in grip strength, core stability and aerial control—skills essential for scaling fort walls and navigating rugged terrain or silently taking out a sentry. These routines emphasized dynamic poses and transitions, cultivating both physical prowess and mental discipline.[12]

In the Maratha Empire, Malkhamb was integrated into akhada-based training regimens for soldiers. The pole served as a surrogate for battlefield obstacles, helping warriors develop reflexes, balance and spatial awareness. Historical accounts suggest that Rani Lakshmibai of Jhansi, along with Nana Saheb and Tantia Tope, practised Malkhamb as part of their martial education.

Malkhamb is often described as an activity that provides 'maximum exercise to maximum muscles in minimum time'. These attributes make Malkhamb not only a physical regimen but also a psychosomatic discipline, akin to yoga and martial

11 Kulkarni, Uday, *Solstice at Panipat: 1761*, Mula-Mutha Publishers, 2011.

12 Deshpande, Sudhir, *Akhadas and Martial Culture in Western India*, Popular Prakashan, 1998.

arts.[13] My school taught Malkhamb too, but I never got the hang of it! Later, at the National Defence Academy, I would often be approached to be part of the Malkhamb display but had to respectfully decline.

Malkhamb is deeply embedded in Maharashtra's cultural identity, often performed during festivals, school events and public demonstrations. Its symbolism extends beyond physicality, representing resilience, tradition and indigenous knowledge systems. As with Lezim, Malkhamb too fosters community bonding and its choreographed routines blend athleticism with aesthetic grace. In 1936, Malkhamb was showcased at the Berlin Olympics as a demonstrative sport, marking its entry into the global arena. Malkhamb's resurgence began in 1958 when it was included in the National Gymnastics Championships in Delhi.[14]

Lezim and Malkhamb are not just calisthenics, but a declaration—of heritage, of discipline, of unity. From Shivaji's akhadas to school playgrounds, from military parades to festival processions, Lezim and Malkhamb continue to shape bodies and minds with their martial rhythm and cultural resonance. In an age of digital distractions and fragmented identities, both offer grounding, and an avenue to move, connect and remember. If Lezim is Maharashtra's heartbeat, echoing through cymbals and footfalls, Malkhamb is its martial ethos, reminding us that tradition, when rooted in strength and shared purpose, never fades but instead becomes a living legacy, in this case of India's martial and cultural heritage.

---

13 Patil, Ramesh, *Malkhamb: The Pole of Power*, Maharashtra State Cultural Board, 2007.

14 Joshi, Meenal, 'Traditional Fitness and Adolescent Health in Maharashtra', *Indian Journal of Physical Education*, Vol. 12, No. 2, 2021.

21

The Missing Man Formation

Flying into the sunset

From the earliest days of aerial warfare, the arrangement of aircraft into coordinated formations has stood as both a tactical imperative and a symbol of precision and discipline. Over time, the design of these formations evolved to meet shifting threats and capabilities, from massed daylight bombing runs defended by interlocking machine-gun fire to modern digital swarms of unmanned aircraft operating independently or integrated seamlessly with manned fighters. This arc began with the iconic bomber box (or combat box), then moved into the dynamic combat spread used by fighters and attack aircraft, and has now entered the revolutionary era of manned-unmanned teaming and the 'loyal wingman' concept.[1]

In the early years of World War II, strategic bombing doctrine rested on a simple premise, namely, that massed bombers flying in tight aerial formations could strike deep into enemy territory with enough concentrated firepower to protect themselves, even without fighter escorts. The US Army Air Forces' solution was the combat box, also known as the staggered formation. In this arrangement, bombers such as the B17s would be arranged vertically and laterally in overlapping

1 Boyne, Walter J., *Beyond the Wild Blue: A History of the U.S. Air Force, 1947-2007*, Thomas Dunne Books, 2007.

layers—lead element, high, low and sometimes even 'low-low', thereby ensuring the security of the formation while at the same time reducing the chances of mid-air collisions. Their defensive .50 calibre machine guns, mounted at various points on the aircraft, covered all approaches, while aligning bomb release paths onto a single target zone. The logic behind this formation was twofold. Defensively, it transformed individual bomber vulnerabilities into collective strength by overlapping fields of fire. Offensively, it concentrated bomb delivery to maximize damage on target.[2] Even as long-range fighter escorts became more prevalent from 1944 onward, the combat box remained in use, valued for its precision and mutual protection.

Then, as aerial combat evolved beyond massed bombers, fighter pilots needed formations that offered both dispersion and mutual support, especially during highspeed engagements or manoeuvres through constrained terrain. This need gave rise to the combat spread, a formation that positioned wingmen separated both laterally and vertically. A wingman is the pilot of the secondary aircraft flying in formation, typically to the side and slightly behind the leader's plane, tasked with providing protection and increasing situational awareness, thus enhancing combat effectiveness by working as a team. (Nowadays, the term is also used in a social context for a person helping out a friend in awkward situations.) 'Wingman' is gender-neutral, but is slowly giving way to 'wingmate'.

When on crosscountry navigation or preparing for combat, pilots would adopt combat spread, separating themselves by several hundred metres vertically and horizontally to improve tactical positioning while avoiding collision risk. Combat spread offered several advantages, namely, a wider observation cone, reduced

---

2 Overy, Richard, *The Bombing War: Europe 1939-1945*, Allen Lane, 2013.

vulnerability to anti-aircraft fire or radar clustering, and flexibility to shift rapidly into offensive or defensive manoeuvres. Wingmen positioned in 'trail' or 'combat cruise' formations, meanwhile, could adapt to terrain or operational constraints by flying behind the lead with limited lateral movement. In air combat, variations of combat spread underpin basic fighter manoeuvres, such as separating into defender 'perch' positions with one aircraft above, one below, to bait and flank attacking opponents.[3]

In combat flying, real formations aren't closely spaced—as in the movies or seen in air shows—and each plane has assigned tasks, including scanning a certain sector of the sky. The Army and Navy too have their own tactical formations, far removed from cinematographic depictions. However, the basic principle remains the same, namely, mutual support, safety and security.

This aerial canvas, always dynamic and symbolic, has long captured mankind's capacity to inspire, to strategize and to honour. The most common and foundational combat formation is the fingerfour (also known as fingertip formation) which features four aircraft arranged like the tips of four fingers (excluding the thumb) when seen from above. It consists of two elements, a Lead element, with the flight leader at the front and a wingman to the rear left, and the Second element, with the element leader to the right and rear of the flight leader, and his wingman, in turn, further to the right and back. This arrangement strikes a balance between flexibility, mutual support and situational awareness, making it historically favoured in air combat.[4] It also forms the basis for some ceremonial variations, the most

3 Shaw, Robert L., *Fighter Combat: Tactics and Maneuvering*, Naval Institute Press, 1985.

4 Spick, Mike, *The Ace Factor: Air Combat and the Role of Situational Awareness*, Naval Institute Press, 1988.

profound of which is the Missing Man formation—a tribute in the skies where a deliberate vacancy in the formation powerfully represents absence. The Missing Man salute evolved over time to become an enduring aerial homage in air forces across the world, including India.

Lost, never forgotten

Although aerial flyovers and displays date back to World War I (when British Squadrons would overfly their airfields so ground crews could tally survivors), a more evocative precedent of today's Missing Man formation first appeared in 1931. At the funeral of Charles W. 'Speed' Holman, the first pilot hired by Northwest Airways, who went on to become the operations manager, four aircraft flew overhead in a broken formation—deliberately leaving a gap, in honour of 'Speed'.[5] This poignant gesture is widely considered the first instance of what evolved into the modern form. This practice, so prominent now in military circles, thus had its roots in the civilian domain. The first recorded flypast to honour a non-Air Force personage was in 1936 to mark the passing of King George V.

By 1938, the practice gained prominence during the funeral of Major General Oscar Westover, the head of the US Army Air Corps. Some fifty fighters and bombers flew overhead, with a blank row of aircraft—almost a Missing Man—symbolically honouring the fallen airman.

The full-fledged modern arrangement typically involves four aircraft in a fingerfour formation. As they pass the salute point, the Second element leader suddenly executes a dramatic

5 Grossnick, Roy A., *United States Naval Aviation 1910-1995*, Naval Historical Center, 1997.

pull-up, or a departure from the formation, symbolizing the absence of the deceased and leaving a silent void in the formation below. Alternative variants include beginning with a missing slot or fading into the sunset (often flown at dusk from the south), richly symbolic of nature. Each variation underscores the metaphor of someone's departure.[6] It possesses ceremonial weight, evoking both respect and loss. Where tactical formations emphasize unity for attack or defence, the Missing Man uses strategic geometry to make loss viscerally visible.

Over time, Missing Man flypasts became ingrained in aerial tradition across air forces and air shows worldwide, and even inspired permanent memorials. The latter include the sculptures at Randolph Air Force Base in Texas, at Joint Base Pearl HarborHickam, Hawaii, and at Valor Park of the National Museum of the US Air Force in Dayton, Ohio, which visually immortalize the formation's sombre shape.[7]

6 Yenne, Bill, *The History of the U.S. Air Force*, Bison Books, 2002.

7 United States Air Force Heritage Program, 'Missing Man Formation Memorials', USAF Historical Research Agency, 2020.

Modern India adopted this aerial tribute relatively recently, yet with profound national and emotional resonance. The first Missing Man formation of the Indian Air Force (IAF) was flown using three MiG-21s shortly after the Kargil War in 1999, an early moment when this Western tradition was incorporated into IAF ceremonial customs. This tradition has since become a central component in honouring India's fallen air warriors. On 18 September 2017, three Sukhoi Su-30MKI fighters executed the Missing Man formation at the funeral of Marshal of the Indian Air Force Arjan Singh in New Delhi, symbolizing the nation's collective sense of loss. Similarly, in February 2019, the IAF's Surya Kiran aerobatics team performed the formation at the Yelahanka airbase in Bengaluru, following the tragic mid-air crash that claimed Wing Commander Sahil Gandhi's life. A Su-30MKI led the flypast, flanked by a Jaguar and a Tejas, which was followed by a slow-speed pass by a Rafale of the French Air Force, in a poignant salute.[8]

Perhaps the most emotionally stirring instance came in May 2019. Air Chief Marshal B.S. Dhanoa, then Chief of Air Staff (CAS), accompanied by Air Marshal R. Nambiar, then Air Officer Commanding-in-Chief (AOC-in-C), Western Air Command, led MiG-21s in the Missing Man formation over Bathinda's Bhisiana Air Force Station. The tribute was to Squadron Leader Ajay Ahuja and other martyrs of Operation Safed Sagar, the IAF's contribution to the Kargil War of 1999. In what may have been the first instance of an IAF CAS and AOC-in-C flying together in such a tribute, the arrow formation showcased a conspicuous gap, an empty space meant to capture the void left by all those

8 Singh, Rahul, ''Missing man' formation marks tribute to IAF pilot Sahil Gandhi', *Hindustan Times*, 21 February 2019, https://tinyurl.com/2s3v38uc. Accessed on 6 December 2025.

who made the supreme sacrifice. This act was repeated the next day in a helicopter formation at Sarsawa, Uttar Pradesh, further underlining its significance. When Air Chief Marshal Dhanoa, once Ahuja's Commanding Officer, led that formation, history and remembrance converged in an unforgettable panorama of MiG-21 silhouettes and the vast sky. This salute transcended mere aviation spectacle, it was a tribute conveyed through the emptiness of silence and spacing.[9] The MiG-21, such a significant part of that occasion, has itself now flown into history with its last sortie completed on 26 September 2025.

Closer in time, after the tragic crash of a Tejas at the Dubai Air Show in November 2025, which claimed the life of Wing Commander Namansh Syal, the US contingent cancelled its show while the Russian Knights flew in the Missing Man formation to honour a fellow aviator, for propriety and compassion know no borders.[10]

Today, formation flying is undergoing further transformation—primarily driven by unmanned capability and artificial intelligence. The enduring concept of the loyal wingman, or Manned-Unmanned Teaming (MUMT), foresees autonomous or remotely piloted drones flying alongside manned aircraft as trusted companions in combat. These Unmanned Combat Aerial Vehicles can perform reconnaissance, electronic warfare, decoy or even offensive roles, reducing risk to human pilots while extending operational reach. Under its Combat Air Teaming System (CATS) programme, Hindustan Aeronautics Ltd is

9 Peri, Dinakar, 'IAF Chief Dhanoa leads 'Missing Man' formation in Mig-21', *The Hindu*, 27 May 2019, https://tinyurl.com/mweursjz. Accessed on 6 December 2025.

10 Bhandari, Isha, ''Brother who didn't return': Russian honours Indian pilot killed in Dubai crash | WATCH', *India TV*, 23 November 2025, https://tinyurl.com/bdeesbn4. Accessed on 6 December 2025.

developing the CATS Warrior, an autonomous loyal wingman concept whereby unmanned or autonomous aircraft operate in tandem with a manned aircraft. Exhibited publicly at Aero India 2025 in Bengaluru, it is intended for operations alongside manned fighters and carriers, underlining India's commitment to MUMT capability development.[11]

From its humble roots in honouring Speed Holman in 1931, the Missing Man formation has soared into the collective lexicon of aerial symbolism. Its evolution, from tactical formation to ceremonial salute, mirrors broader shifts in air power and the value of human and technological synergy. In India, the formation enriches national memory, binding air crew, leadership and the public in shared recognition and homage. As we continue advancing into an era of drones and autonomous wingmen, the silent space in a Missing Man formation remains a powerful reminder that every such formation, above all, honours those who are missing yet forever present in spirit.

11 Aroor, Shiv, and Shivani Sharma, 'CATS Warrior redefines unmanned combat aviation, know all about it', *India Today*, 10 February 2025, https://tinyurl.com/mr28y67u. Accessed on 6 December 2025.

SECTION VI

TOAST TO TRADITION

22

Messes and Wardrooms

Heritage is served

Amid resplendent regimental silver, camaraderie and ritual walk hand in hand. Meals are shared over laughter and banter, formal dinner nights are steeped in pride and precedence, regimental gatherings foster brotherhood and bonhomie, and the occasional ladies' get-togethers bring warmth to halls celebrated for their tradition. Feted in military circles as architectural and cultural relics, they often preserve colonial design, old furnishings, trophies, emblems and a sense of continuity that links to India's history under the British and before.[1]

This continuity is intentional. Many of India's colonial military traditions survive not only in ceremonies, uniforms and names but also in buildings and institutions that continue to serve much the same purpose they were meant for in earlier centuries. Among these, one of the most evocative is the Officers' Mess: the home away from home for commissioned officers in the Army, Air Force or Navy.

The word 'mess', by the way, does not have any connection to disorder or untidiness. It comes from the Old French *mes*, meaning a portion of food or a course of a meal, and that in turn comes via Late Latin *missus* (something 'sent' or 'put' on

1 Chopra, Preeti, *A Joint Enterprise: Indian Elites and the Making of British Bombay*, University of Minnesota Press, 2011.

the table), from *mittere* (to send/put/place). In England, around the 14th century, *mess* meant 'a supply or provision of food for one meal' or a serving, especially cooked or liquid food. As time progressed, there came about one meaning which referred to a group of people who ate together. By the 15th or early 16th century, in military or naval contexts, *mess* was being used to describe those who shared meals together and, later, the place itself where they dined.[2]

The 'messy' meaning—untidy, disorganized, or chaotic—came much later. That sense seems to derive from the idea of mixed or blended things (as in a 'mess' of food, for example a stew or porridge) that are less neat or refined. Over the 18th and 19th centuries, the notion of 'mixed food' expanded in usage, and from there, figuratively, to any jumbled or disorderly condition. Thus, what was once a neutral or positive word (shared meals, community) took on a negative connotation when applied in

2 Mess, *Oxford English Dictionary*, Oxford University Press, 2023.

different contexts. Which is why the word 'Mess' should always be capitalized to distinguish it from its messy counterpart![3]

Another popular claim is that *MESS* is an acronym for Members of Equal Social Status which is often used to explain away the word 'Mess' without delving into its historical roots. This is not supported by linguistic or historical evidence. In fact, there is no indication that the word ever originated as an acronym. Rather, this kind of explanation is yet another example of a *backronym*—a phrase invented after the fact to give meaning to the word. This backronym might have originated from the fact that in the Officers' Mess, members can let their hair down and juniors and seniors can rub shoulders in convivial settings, far removed from the strict hierarchy that prevails at formal parades. In fact, the Commanding Officer (CO) is just another member of the Mess, the President of the Mess Committee being the Second-in-Command (2iC), to reflect this egalitarian status. Linguists consider such musings akin to folktales: appealing, but not historically accurate.[4]

Its evolution aside, the term itself is not uniform across the three Services. While the Army and Air Force use the term Officers' Mess, the Navy typically uses 'wardroom' for its officer dining and social quarters. The Wardroom carries with it its own history and tradition, shaped by life at sea as well as on shore.

The term *wardroom* is believed to have evolved from *wardrobe*, a shipboard compartment used in Britain's Royal Navy in the 18th century. That compartment stored prizes of war (booty, valuables) and was located near the officers' cabins. When the wardrobe was empty, especially during long voyages

3 Crystal, David, *The Stories of English*, Penguin Books, 2004.

4 Liberman, Anatoly, *Origin Uncertain: Unraveling the Mysteries of Etymology*, Oxford University Press, 2024.

without prize captures or during the outward journey, officers began using it as a place to dine, relax, read and socialize. Gradually, it transformed into a dedicated space for officers' meals and gatherings, and the name 'wardrobe room' came to be associated with that use. Over time, the 'robe' part was dropped or merged in usage, leading to 'wardroom'.[5]

On a warship, the Wardroom is strictly reserved for commissioned officers, with enlisted sailors or ratings dining in the Messes or Mess Decks. The Wardroom thus serves multiple functions beyond dining, doubling as a lounge, meeting room, social space, and sometimes hosting briefings or ceremonies. Its furnishings, decor and traditions often reflect naval history, including the ship's or squadron's battle honours, crest and memorabilia, much like land-based Messes. It also reflects the isolation and self-sufficiency of shipboard life, as seen in its layout, proximity to officers' cabins, shared facilities and space constraints. By tradition, the Captain of the ship dines by himself in his cabin and only enters the Wardroom when specially invited. This tradition also evolved to keep the Wardroom—to use a modern term—'user-friendly', where officers can grab a quick bite before or after a watch without being tied down by the formality that the Captain's presence would necessitate.[6]

Food, drink and a dash of history

Starting from colonial times, the Mess was regarded as a badge of status. Having a good Mess was a matter of prestige, and the standard of a unit could often be gauged from the standard of

---

5 Rodger, N.A.M., *The Command of the Ocean: A Naval History of Britain, 1649-1815*, Penguin Books, 2004.

6 Till, Geoffrey, *Seapower: A Guide for the Twenty-First Century*, Routledge, 2013.

its Officers' Mess. As one historical account from the mid-19th century notes, officers in Regiments tried to ensure cleanliness, good furniture, matting for floors, ornamented prints on walls, trays and cups and spoons of quality, to distinguish their Mess in comfort and style. Over time, some Messes became known for their exceptional interiors, gardens, traditions and artefacts.[7]

This legacy lives on in several historic messes. One such enduring example is Kitchener's House (now renamed Manekshaw House), one of the oldest surviving Mess buildings in India that still functions as an Officers' Mess. It is located inside Fort William (now renamed Vijay Durg) in Kolkata (earlier Calcutta). The building was constructed in 1771 as a blockhouse (a fortified residence) for what was called the Fortress Assault Company. Over time its use evolved. Lord Richard Wellesley, the then Governor-General of India, stayed there over 1789–1803. With the British capital shifting from Calcutta to Delhi in 1911, it was repurposed as the Officers' Mess of the Bengal Presidency.

However, this building was named much later after Field Marshal Lord Horatio Herbert Kitchener, the First Earl of Khartoum, who resided here as Commander-in-Chief from 1902 to 1909. Field Marshal Manekshaw, after whom the building is now named, was also the Army Commander of the Eastern Command over 1964–69, but he stayed at Senapati Bhawan in Alipore, the designated official residence. I too had the honour of residing in this most iconic of residences during 2018–19.

Manekshaw House is still in use today as the Officers' Mess for the Bengal Sub Area of the Indian Army. Its architecture blends Gothic and Georgian styles and it remains well maintained, though access is restricted as it falls within the garrison, though

7 Roy, Kaushik, *Military Manpower, Armies and Warfare in South Asia*, Routledge, 2015.

there is some accommodation for heritage walks.[8] During such walks, you may also come across the 'Time Gun', manufactured in 1756, which was fired daily from the riverbank at precisely 1300h to indicate the time to ships navigating the Hooghly River. With the advent of modern communication systems, the gun fell into disuse and was shifted to Kitchener's House in 1938.[9]

Another very old building associated with the Mess tradition is Kota House in New Delhi. Built in 1938 by Maharao Umed Singh II, and designed in Art Deco style by architects from Bombay, it was acquired by the British government in India and used in various ways (as a hospital during World War II, a hostel, etc.). It changed hands several times and in 1983, it was transferred from the Army to the Indian Navy, which converted it into the Naval Officers' Mess Annexe, known by the acronym NOMA. Though it is not as old as Manekshaw House, its use by the Navy and its well-kept gardens and colonial/Art Deco architecture make it another striking Mess.[10]

Yet another one, with both lineage and charm, is the Bombay Sappers Officers' Mess in Kirkee (now reverting to its original name Khadki), Pune. Built between March 1906 and April 1907 by officers and soldiers of the Royal Engineers (Bombay Sappers), this Mess has remarkable features: colonial stone masonry, wooden pillars, lush gardens, shoulder-high elephant tusks displayed at the entrance, and antique-style *pankha*s (large cloth ceiling fans operated by hand by bearers from an adjoining

---

8 Ray, Dalia, *Fort William and Calcutta Maidan: The British Heritage of Calcutta*, Punthi Pustak, 2021.

9 Sengupta, Kamalika, 'Here is an Exclusive Peek into British-era Kitchener House of Fort William in Kolkata', *News18*, 9 November 2021, https://tinyurl.com/mwxj5s3u. Accessed on 6 December 2025.

10 'Kota House, 1938', *Deco In Delhi*, https://tinyurl.com/3hyk7epr. Accessed on 4 December 2025.

room), which have been kept functional though obviously are not used. The Mess is special partly because the officers themselves, historically, have contributed (financially and in maintenance) to its construction and preservation.

This tradition of contribution is hardly surprising given that Messes are more than just heritage landmarks. Even today, officers, on first joining their units, are expected to make a one-time voluntary contribution from their monthly pay to the Mess—not because it lacks funds but to instil a feeling of ownership regarding the institution. Messes serve as centres of social life for officers—formal dining, mess dinners, regimental or squadron ceremonies, meetings, guest receptions, social mingling and lodging—hence the phrase 'home away from home'. Many Messes preserve ritual: saluting, designated places, dress codes, mess plates or insignia, portraits of past Commanders or Colonels, trophies, swords and glittering silverware. These practices reinforce regimental pride and the bond between officers.

This explains why Officers' Messes have retained their central role in an officer's life. Today, every major unit has one, and many heritage buildings continue to be preserved. The British architectural influence—verandahs, large dining halls, colonial stone or masonry, and wooden pillars—remains visible. Heritage walks in places like Vijay Durg now include Manekshaw House among the sights unavoidably linked to India's colonial past yet still in military use, a living museum. The preservation of interiors, artefacts, and the structure itself (even if not all rooms are used exactly as before) helps to connect present officers with their predecessors.

While heritage Messes retain their historic character, newer Messes have evolved to reflect contemporary values and post-Independence history. They are more modern and utilitarian, with electricity replacing pankhas, modernization of kitchens, more diverse decor, inclusion of officers from diverse nationalities, and changes in formality, mess plates or insignia. Some Messes have become more open in membership rules or in guest policy; some have expanded to include families or civilian guests. The social ritual remains strong, however, with strict rules and etiquette.[11]

Officers' Messes in India are both living institutions and historical artefacts. Buildings like Manekshaw House, Khadki's Bombay Sappers Mess and Kota House illustrate how architecture, ritual and military tradition intertwine. They showcase colonial-era styles (stone, wood, decorative detailing) while demonstrating how such institutions continue to matter, whether during daily meals, formal dinners or in preserving regimental and naval identity. The naval Wardroom branches off from the army Mess tradition in structure and culture, shaped by shipboard life and naval hierarchy, but shares in the same underlying values of equality among officers, discipline, ceremony and social bonds.

The story of the word *mess* itself reminds us how the language of tradition evolves. What began as a simple notion of food or portion later expanded to describe a group that eats together, the place where it eats, and eventually even as a metaphor for disorder. The 'messy' sense is secondary—but it is also part of the history. Meanwhile, the myth of MESS as an acronym may be comforting or poetic, but scholarship shows it is not historical. Instead, the word is older than any such acronym, and its meaning has been shaped gradually through centuries of use.

---

11 Chopra, Preeti, *A Joint Enterprise: Indian Elites and the Making of British Bombay*, University of Minnesota Press, 2011.

In a way, the Officers' Mess is more than just a dining hall. It is a repository of recollection, status, ritual and belonging. For many officers, serving as well as retired, entering the Mess, seeing the portraits of past COs and gallantry award winners (perhaps even your own), the silver, the trophies, the old paintings of bygone battles, relics like strapped ceiling fans, courtyards and manicured gardens—all these elements reinforce the continuity of something that is greater than the individual. And that is the Service as part of a tradition, a lineage, a record that is lived every day in food, drink, conversation, laughter and remembrance, a daily addition to the pages of history.

23

Do Bottle, *Teen* Glass

Shaken, stirred and in high spirits

Leave, whether annual or casual, is an indispensable part of the yearly management plan. Towards the end of the year, all officers are requested to submit their leave choices to enable preparation of the following year's leave plan, a task usually undertaken by the unit Second-in-Command (2iC). This is to ensure that officers get a break every few months while still maintaining the unit's desired strength throughout the year, particularly when important events are scheduled.

In the early years of my career, when there used to be fifteen to sixteen officers posted to a unit against an authorized strength of twenty-plus, this exercise was quite complex, ensuring back-up at all levels. For example, not more than 50 per cent of Company Commanders could be on leave at any point of time, and the Commanding Officer (CO) and 2iC obviously couldn't be away simultaneously either. It was all the more necessary sometimes, because proper accommodation for all officers was scarce. It helped if not too many officers were present in the unit, as sometimes we had to stay three-to-a-room! Those days are long gone, and units now have to contend with a posted strength of thirteen to fifteen officers in field areas and barely eight to ten officers in peace stations.[1]

---

1 Francis, J., *Short Stories from the History of the Indian Army Since August 1947*, KW Publishers, 2013.

Many officers have spent hours poring over the yearly Army Postal Service (APS) calendar in which Sundays and holidays are marked in red, figuring out how best to schedule their vacation with the maximum of prefixes and suffixes to extend the leave as much as possible. I dare say that the APS calendar is studied with more care and concentration than any map or training manual! And the plan has to be made with utmost secrecy lest some other officer get the same idea and bung in his/her leave application first. It is first come, first served.

Putting in the leave application is only the first step, though; it has to go through the gauntlet—securing recommendation from the Adjutant and 2iC—before final approval by the CO. The last is a mere formality, if the previous two worthies have done due diligence. The Adjutant is the tougher nut to crack, as she has to be convinced that there are no odd jobs pending against the officer's name.

So, here is how it goes.

Adequate number of officers remaining? Check.
Duty officers form filled out and submitted? Check.
Monthly/annual stock taking board carried out and submitted? Check.
Not a member or presiding officer of any pending court of inquiry? Check.

Arrangements for performance of duty in absence? Hmm...that's a tough one. Better leave it for the 2iC to decide, especially if it is likely to fall on the shoulders of someone senior to her. Why take *panga* (mess) with a senior officer unnecessarily? A final glance and a flamboyant signature later, the application is sent off.

The 2iC then scrutinizes the leave application as if it were a top-secret document with grave implications for national security, all the while with the officer squirming in the chair opposite. A simple 'the leave applied for is as per the approved leave plan' won't do. Extreme extenuating circumstances have to be conjured, a true test of the officer's imagination. The 2iC is not bereft of ideas either.

> Have the audit board proceedings been submitted/signed?
> Check.
> What about that renovation work in the Officers' Mess?
> (Oh, bloody hell, had completely forgotten about it.) 'It's on track, sir, you'll be able to see it soon.'
> 'Bloody well hope so.'

The application is then signed with a flourish and the office runner summoned to put up the file to the CO. The 2iC then invariably puts the question, '*Do* bottle, *teen* glass?'

Ridiculous blends with sublime

Two bottles of beer to be shared between three officers, the 2iC, the Adjutant and the officer who had requested the leave (who is the host on the occasion), was a custom prevalent in many units. Once the leave was sanctioned, the three officers would repair to the Officers' Mess and share a tale or two over a glass of beer. Why not three bottles for three officers, one might well ask? Because it was not about drinking but about sharing. About fostering a spirit of camaraderie in the informal setting of the Officers' Mess, where distinctions of rank are set aside. Where ideas can be exchanged freely and frankly, especially since the CO is not around, and purposely so, in spite of the fact that it is the CO who is the final approving authority.[2] It is an informal mechanism where the officers can share their woes and seek advice from their more experienced seniors.

In a hierarchical organization where rank and discipline often define interpersonal relations, the act of sharing a couple of bottles of beer reminds everyone involved that the officers, regardless of their rank or position, are united in their shared history as part of that unit. It also serves to humanize the otherwise strict hierarchical relationships within the unit, breaking down barriers, however temporarily, and create a space where seniority becomes less important than the common heritage.[3]

An officer might confide that he gets stressed out when he goes on leave because his parents keep trying to find a match for him, arranging numerous high teas to introduce prospective

---

2 Arora, R.K., and Henry Roach, *Customs and Etiquette in the Services*, Natraj Publishers, 2009.

3 Raghavan, V.R., *Soldiering and Society: Military Ethics and Civil-Military Relations*, Penguin India, 2015.

brides. Sometimes it could be the exact opposite: the officer has found a suitable partner, the couple is in love, but the respective sets of parents are opposed to the match. Parents' illnesses, property disputes, problems around children's education, nothing is off-limits. Such informal interaction and counselling help both ways, building mutual trust and *esprit de corps* as well as an escape valve for the officer to vent his feelings in the relative anonymity of the unit, without offending any close friends or relatives.[4]

It may sound like serious stuff, but the ritual is not without its share of absurdity, given the entire rigmarole involved in something as simple as getting one's leave sanctioned—from filling out the application to getting the leave certificate, an all-important document without which one would be declared absent without leave. It is the Army's version of bureaucracy, a blend of the ridiculous and the sublime (after all, what can be more sublime than a chilled glass of beer on a hot summer afternoon?), which is best appreciated by those who have been part of the process.[5]

Unfortunately, in today's fast-paced world, this custom is fast disappearing. In the era of social media and remote interactions, it is all the more important that such small gestures are preserved/revived for the greater good. Not only in the Army but, perhaps in a different *avatar*, in all walks of life, to increase human interaction and bonhomie, reduce stress and restore work-life balance, which seems to be increasingly absent. So, if you ever hear the phrase 'Do bottle, teen glass',

4 Mason, Philip, *A Matter of Honour: An Account of the Indian Army, Its Officers and Men*, Natraj Publishers, 2004.

5 Banerjee, Arjun, *The Bureaucratic Soldier: Rituals and Routines in the Indian Army*, SAGE Publications, 2016.

smile good-naturedly, recollect its lineage and join in if possible.

'Two bottles, three glasses' is more than just an archaic custom; it is a reminder that the Army, despite its hard-boiled exterior, is ultimately made up of ordinary men and women with their usual strengths and weaknesses, united by the uniform and sworn to uphold the honour of the Regiment. It also shows that even in the most formal and regimented organizations, there is room for merriment, shared confidences and an occasional beer—or two.

24

Rumbustious Rum

Sips of sweet nectar of the tropics

'Fifteen men on the Dead Man's Chest—
Yo-ho-ho, and a bottle of rum!
Drink and the devil had done for the rest—
Yo-ho-ho, and a bottle of rum!'

I wonder if the longevity of this verse somehow mirrors the quality of the drink in question, particularly its remarkable capacity to transcend time and geography. Few literary works have lines that outlive the very stories they belong to, and this verse about pirates from *Treasure Island* written by Robert Louis Stevenson in 1883 is just one of them. This stanza was expanded into a full-fledged poem called 'Derelict' by Young Ewing Allison, published in 1891, who extended the song to include vivid verses with gruesome pirate imagery. Across generations, it has been widely adopted and reimagined in numerous other works of art, media and popular culture. Since pirates mostly operated in regions like the Caribbean and plundered ships, including those carrying rum or its ingredients, coupled with pirate-friendly ports which were also centres for the rum trade, this inexorably linked the two in popular imagination.[1]

1 Stevenson, Robert Louis, *Treasure Island*, Cassell & Company, 1883. Allison, Young Ewing, 'Derelict', *Louisville Courier-Journal*, 1891.

This rum-pirate connection comes from a mix of historical facts, latter-day myth and romanticizing. In much the same way, rum has traditionally been associated with the Armed Forces, in particular with the Army. Its mention brings to mind macho, moustachioed men dancing around a blazing bonfire, downing peg after peg of this sweet nectar while singing patriotic songs. Nothing could be further from the truth.

In fact, the story behind the spread of rum has more to do with Britain's Royal Navy (and other navies) that began issuing daily rations of rum (or rum and water mixes) to sailors. Rum was more durable than most drinks, and safer than water stored on board for long periods, which could go stale or become contaminated. Its high alcohol content inhibited the growth of bacteria and mould, which were common problems with other liquids stored on ships. Life at sea was hard and rum helped with morale, provided something to trade or barter with, and, mixed with water or other ingredients (like citrus or sugar), could make grog, which helped make water more palatable and safer. It was also served to sailors to protect them against scurvy.[2] So, devil's brew or medicinal, is for you to decide!

When sugar was introduced to the New World, the Caribbean Islands and Latin America following Christopher Columbus's voyages, its production became the mainstay of plantation economies. This, in turn, produced large quantities of molasses as part of the refining process, which when fermented and distilled became a strong alcoholic beverage. So strong, in fact, that a reference to this 'sweet nectar' from 1651 describes it as '...rumbullion, alias Kill-Devil...a hot, hellish, and terrible

---

2 Williams, Ian, *Rum: A Social and Sociable History of the Real Spirit of 1776*, Lyons Press, 2005.

liquor...made of sugar-canes distilled.'[3]

This is also possibly the origin of the moniker 'rum' given to this distillate, though several other theories exist. Some think 'rum' might derive from *saccharum*, the Latin for sugar, since sugar and cane products are involved. In early British slang, 'rum' meant anything that was odd, curious or of high quality, so perhaps the name evolved from that. Whatever the case, by 1654 the word was in common usage to describe this type of liquor originating from the Caribbean.[4]

This exotic drink soon reached Indian shores courtesy of the Royal Navy, and large-scale sugar production in India began under colonial rule, with sugar refineries established in Bengal and elsewhere to supply sugar to the British. It followed logically that the molasses produced as the by-product would get converted to rum, also for supply to the British. In 1805, a British industrialist named John Maxwell founded the first distillery of the subcontinent in Kanpur to supply alcoholic beverages specifically to the British Army. He brought in a specialist by the name of Robert Carew who bought the company from Maxwell; this gave birth to Carew & Co. in 1847. Another important distillery was founded by Edward Abraham Dyer, a British businessman (and father of the infamous General Reginald Dyer of Jallianwala Bagh notoriety) in the mid19th century with breweries and then distilleries in the Solan hills, as was yet another distillery founded by H.G. Meakin. These merged some years later to become Dyer Meakin and Co. Ltd, which had a number of

3 Curtis, Wayne, *And a Bottle of Rum: A History of the New World in Ten Cocktails*, Crown Publishing, 2006.

4 Williams, Ian, *Rum: A Social and Sociable History of the Real Spirit of 1776*, Lyons Press, 2005.

distilleries/breweries set up under British ownership. They played an important role in domestic alcohol manufacture, including rum, whisky and beer.[5]

After Independence, the liquor industry was reorganized under Indian entrepreneurs. In due course, Dyer Meakin became Mohan Meakin Ltd, one of the most well-known companies in India, with the baton passing to N.N. Mohan in 1949. One of their most iconic rum brands is Old Monk. It was introduced in December 1954 by his son Ved Rattan Mohan, a retired Colonel, as a tribute to the Benedictine monks he had encountered and admired during a trip to Europe. Later, his brother, Brigadier Kapil Mohan (a teetotaller himself), took over the leadership of the company, and their understanding of what soldiers might prefer or what suits 'life in uniform' helped not only in shaping brand strategy but also in entrenching its position within the Army.[6] Another equally famous brand is the Hercules XXX, produced exclusively for Army use. These two iconic brands survive to the present day.

Ritual, ration and regimental recall

Considering that everything in the Army is a parade—the early morning physical training is PT parade, a visit to a place of worship is Mandir/Masjid/Gurudwara or Church parade, pay parade occurs at the end of the month, and unruly soldiers are sometimes subjected to an unofficial punishment, *kambal* parade, by having a blanket thrown over them and being given a few swift blows—it is no surprise that there is an utterly

5 Corporate History, Mohan Meakin Archives, Mohan Meakin Ltd, https://tinyurl.com/2t2hvf2m. Accessed on 3 December 2025.

6 Ibid.

endearing legacy, the 'rum parade'. Its origins can be traced to as far back as World War I, when British and Commonwealth troops had a 'rum ration' of 2.5 fluid ounces (approximately 70 ml) daily in the trenches, to be consumed under supervision to prevent abuse.[7]

Amid concerns about including spirits as part of rations, Sir Hugh Rose, as Commander-in-Chief, India, over 1860–65, reduced the daily rum ration in India from 'two drams to one per day' because of health concerns in a tropical climate. Over time, this was standardized to 60 ml (one large peg) two or three times a week at the discretion of the local commander. The local commander, usually the Commanding Officer, could also authorize 'special issue' on specific occasions like the unit's Raising Day (anniversary) or if the unit had done extremely well in some professional or sports competitions.[8] These issues of rum were, and are, strictly controlled and handed out at lunch or dinner in peace locations, but only at lunch time in forward areas.

The rum parade is simple yet complicated—if this can be conveyed. On the given day and hour, usually before mealtimes, all the men queue in a 'fall-in' in front of their respective Company cook-houses (*langar*), where the Company Quartermaster (CQM) has already set up shop—a table with bottles of rum and a peg measure. He is joined by the Company senior Junior Commissioned Officer (JCO) and, on occasion, the Company Commander. One by one, each jawan steps forward and signs against his name in the nominal roll as acknowledgement of having received his 'tot', but only after the senior JCO has verified

7 Curtis, Wayne, *And a Bottle of Rum: A History of the New World in Ten Cocktails*, Crown Publishing, 2006.

8 Williams, Ian, *Rum: A Social and Sociable History of the Real Spirit of 1776*, Lyons Press, 2005.

whether the individual is a 'drinker' or 'non-drinker'. Everything in the Army is streamlined thus—either you are a 'meater' (non-vegetarian) or you are a 'non-meater' (vegetarian). It is simple yet complicated.

Once given the okay, the CQM pours the peg into the proffered glass and then watches hawkeyed to ensure it is downed then and there. No taking it away to sip at leisure with your buddies! The jawan then moves on to the langar for the day's meal. In a few cases, the jawan might dilute the drink from a bottle of water kept handy but, even then, it has to be consumed on the spot. This elaborate process was designed to ensure that no one drinks more than his authorized quota. Jawans have been known to request a 'non-drinker' buddy to get in line as a proxy, but the ploy has never succeeded. The senior JCO knows exactly who drinks and who does not, and in any case the peg has to be drunk on the spot.

The only beneficiary is the CQM who collects the spillage from the peg measure and shares a quiet drink (or two) with the senior JCO afterwards. The only losers are the non-drinkers who do not benefit from the entire exercise but, since a parade is a parade, have to be present.

This elaborate exercise has other benefits too. The Company Commander gets to see his jawans face to face and exchange a few words of greeting or enquire about the man's or his family's well-being. The jawans, too, get an opportunity to reach out directly to their officer, without having to go through intermediaries like the Section or Platoon Commander. It helps the Company Commander stay connected and have his finger on the pulse of the command. Is everything tickety-boo, '*chardi kalan*', or are there undercurrents of tension? There is certainly a method in the madness.

Apart from its military roots, rum has inspired a diverse array of songs across genres and eras. The most popular is probably 'Rum and Coca-Cola', a calypso song recorded by the Andrews sisters which gained widespread popularity in the US in the 1940s. Little wonder then that the drink itself has timeless appeal: Rum and Coke with a slice of lemon on a hot summer day is incomparable.

Rum's connection with the Army is a mix of colonial legacy, logistical/market factors, culture and identity. Leaders with military backgrounds in rum-producing firms seemed to understand intimately what soldiers would accept and prefer—cost, flavour, strength, reliability. Rum thus occupies a space that is part practical, part symbolic—a commodity, a comfort, a symbol of shared hardship or shared rest. And while some of the more colourful stories (rum for mules, for example) hover between folklore and recollection, they reflect how deeply ingrained rum is in the imagination of soldiers and veterans alike. And what about the image of soldiers dancing around camp bonfires, bottle in hand? Alas, that too is a stereotype propagated by the celluloid world—and gravely unjust to the uniformed fraternity.

Hic, hic, hooray!

25

P.P.C.

A farewell to arms

In the grand, romanticized and chequered history of military protocols and expressions, few phrases are as uniquely French and delightfully quaint as *pour prendre congé*, or more simply just 'P.P.C'. These three simple little words may sound relatively innocuous at first but once the layers of the historical and cultural context are uncovered, it reveals an amusing, occasionally baffling, and altogether charming tale that spans centuries of rich military tradition and meaning, along with a dash of French flair and insouciance. Roughly translated as 'to take leave', it was in common usage till quite recently, when customs, traditions and etiquette passed down from British times still played a major role in garrison life. Although today the phrase is largely unheard, a relic of a bygone era, it once played a central role in military life, particularly when officers were moving out on posting to a new station or unit.[1]

According to historical records, *pour prendre congé* first appeared in military culture during the reign of King Louis XIV or *le Roi Soleil* (the Sun King) of France. The 17th century was a time of strict codes of conduct in both civilian and military life, with protocols dictating nearly every action a person could

1 Chandler, David, *The Art of Warfare in the Age of Marlborough*, Spellmount, 1990.

undertake, especially for those in uniform or in the service of the Crown. France, with its elaborate court systems, was the epitome of royal grandeur and social stratification. Noblemen, officers and even common soldiers had to follow a very defined set of manners, speech and rituals. The phrase *pour prendre congé* began as a formal way for officers to request time off from their superiors, and it was often part of an elaborate set of rituals when an officer needed to leave their post temporarily, for whatever reason, whether personal, health or some other need for respite.[2]

By the late 18th and 19th centuries, this formality became so entrenched in military culture that it evolved into a more specific expression of departure for when officers were either being transferred, retiring or bidding farewell to their comrades. The exact moment when P.P.C. became a staple in the Visitors' Books of Officers' Messes is hard to pinpoint, as these books were, by nature, informal historical records. Yet, the act of leaving was never a casual affair. There was ceremony involved, and P.P.C. became part of the lexicon of military life, ensuring that an officer's departure was always handled with due respect, pomp and ceremony. Just as the military expected proper attention to rank and formality in official matters, it expected the same in matters of social conduct.[3]

Signing off, updated

One of the most recognizable markers of this social etiquette is the 'Visitors' Book' maintained by every Officers' Mess.

2 Vigarello, Georges, *A History of Manners: From the Renaissance to the Present*, Polity Press, 2008.

3 Keegan, John, *The Face of Battle*, Penguin Books, 1976.

A leather-bound book, it is polished to a fine sheen, with silver corner trims and a silver plate on the cover's centre bearing the unit's name and other details. It is usually placed near the main entrance of the Mess on an elegant table. Apart from the Visitors' Book, the table also displays framed photographs of the Commanding Officer of the unit and of the Colonel of the Regiment, so that everyone knows without asking the names of these important appointees/officers. The Colonel of the Regiment is an officer of the Regiment elected through a democratic process, who acts as mentor for the Regiment as a whole, looking after the interest of all the units that comprise the Regiment. He could be of any rank from Brigadier to General, but is referred to as the Colonel of the Regiment, even wearing the rank badges of a Colonel when the occasion so demands. I had the privilege of being the Colonel of the Regiment for the Sikh Light Infantry as well as the honorary Colonel of the Regiment for the Bombay Sappers.

The Visitors' Book is started when a unit is raised or established, with new volumes added over the years. Every visitor to the Officers' Mess, on the first visit, is expected to enter his or her rank, name, unit and date of visit. On subsequent visits, no such entry is made, unless a number of years have elapsed in between. These volumes are thus a historical record as well as a living legacy of all those who would have ever been associated with that unit. Browsing the names in the Visitors' Book is like taking a trip down memory lane—when Generals were young Majors or Captains, and Captains young subalterns. In essence, the Visitors' Book serves as both a digest of military personnel and a reminder of the ties that bind officers.

All officers, on first reporting to a unit, also make an entry in the Visitors' Book as a formal way of announcing their arrival at the station. Thereafter, unit officers make an entry only during the 'dining out'—the farewell function—when they are officially posted out of the station and cease to remain members of that Mess. This farewell entry is not merely a casual goodbye but a final, formal acknowledgement of one's service in that unit and a gesture of respect to the comrades being left behind. In days gone by, apart from the personal particulars, the officer would also enter the name of the unit he was being posted to and, in the Remarks column, would write 'P.P.C.' to signify that the association with the present unit was coming to an end. Customarily, that was the only time an officer was allowed to make an entry in the Remarks column, which was otherwise reserved for notings of the President of the Mess Committee (PMC), usually the Second-in-Command of the unit.

In earlier times, when traditions ruled the roost, the Visitors' Book would be perused by the PMC at regular intervals. In the Remarks column, which was meant exclusively for this purpose, the PMC would record directions regarding the officers and other callers who had visited: who should be made honorary members, who should be added to the invitee list for future events, who should be treated as guests (i.e., not to be billed), and so on.[4] It was not supposed to be a column for visitors to pen their thoughts on the standards of the Mess and how much they had enjoyed their stay, and sometimes even vent their feelings over some incident or the other! For that, there is a separate suggestions book, which is also perused by the PMC, and action taken—usually a *shabaash* (commendation) to the Mess staff.

---

4 Heathcote, T.A., *The Military in British India: The Development of British Land Forces in South Asia 1600-1947*, Manchester University Press, 1995.

With these traditions almost forgotten, the full form of P.P.C. has faded from memory as well. The more modern and colloquial version of P.P.C. is *pi, paa ke chale*, a jocular version of 'let's drink and go' or 'I've had my fill, thanks, I'm off'. In a manner of speaking, it is almost akin to taking leave as per the old customs, but with a modern twist. It is not uncommon to hear officers jokingly calling out 'PPC!' in a slightly inebriated manner when leaving a gathering, signalling their departure with an exaggerated elegance, much to the amusement of their colleagues, and with knowing glances exchanged among the ladies. And much as we may chuckle at the formality of it all, there's something undeniably charming about the idea of a military world where officers were required to make their departures as grand as their entrances, that too in a foreign language!

Young officers, more often than not caught up in the humdrum of Company administration, have their own take. If asked what P.P.C. stands for, they are more likely to offer the very mundane 'papad, pickle and condiment', a far cry from the grandeur that *pour prendre congé* evokes. Not their fault, though, because there is indeed a monetary allowance for P.P.C.—papad, pickle, condiments—entitled to every jawan as part of the authorized rations. Drawing the allowance, accounting for it and making sure it is judiciously used does take up a lot of time and effort, so it is quite reasonable for them to respond with the first thing that comes to mind. In this sense, the phrase P.P.C. has morphed from a serious, formal request to a light-hearted reminder of a bygone era of military life.[5]

---

5 Liberman, Anatoly, 'Acronyms and Folk Etymology', *Oxford Etymologist*, Oxford University Press blog, 2019.

P.P.C. has faded into the realm of nostalgia. It is now the sort of phrase heard only in historical re-enactments, or perhaps among old-school officers reminiscing about the good old days while sipping their Scotch. Quite often, it is also invoked in jest, with younger officers referring to it in its more humorous avatars.

When I was due to superannuate in April 2022 on completion of my tenure as the Chief of the Army Staff, I was also dined out from the Army Battle Honours Mess on S.P. Marg in Delhi. At the entrance to the ante-room and the adjoining dining room, which is on the first floor, is an ornate wooden table, with a photo of the President of India, our Commander-in-Chief, and the Visitors' Book. Looking down from above are portraits of Field Marshal K.M. Cariappa and Field Marshal S.H.F.J. Manekshaw, smiling benignly as if still supervising matters.

After a most elaborate dinner hosted by my successor, General Manoj Pande, I was graciously ushered to the Visitors' Book table.

There, I made my final entry, ending with P.P.C. It encapsulated everything the Army had taught me to value: respect, decorum, and the inevitability of personal and professional transitions, of letting go with grace and never looking back.

Visitor's Book

Date	Name & Address	Remarks
28 Apr 22	Gen M M Naravane COAS	PPC

And with that, dear readers, I now take leave.

Acknowledgements

Right at the outset, I must acknowledge the role of Dr Shashi Tharoor for being the spark behind this book. Sometimes a fleeting moment or comment can ignite the mind with an idea that continues to agitate the mind until put to rest—in this case through this book. But ideas are not enough. It needs someone to perceive the potential to convert that idea into something tangible, and for that I have to thank Rupa Publications and the entire team for extending whole-hearted support. My special thanks to Yamini Chowdhury for her enthusiastic support. Being a former Army officer herself, she perhaps found the idea as intriguing as I did.

Hunting for more stories—I initially had only about a dozen—I turned to family and friends for more such nuggets that I could expand upon. In this endeavour, I must once again thank Yamini (and, I suspect, her husband) as well as my daughters, Isha and Amala, amongst others, for their valuable inputs. Equally important was the feedback on what not to write about, usually because it had already been written about. As a result, I feel each chapter is unique in its own way.

Half-way through writing the book, I thought it could do with a few illustrations. I envisaged one at the beginning of each chapter, to maintain the light-hearted flavour as well as to set the tone for what the chapter was going to be about. For this I roped in my son-in-law, Simon Massey, who is proficient in all art forms, be it dancing, theatre, photography or sketching. All the illustrations are his and his alone, and I feel that they add considerable value as well as a humorous touch to the book, the illustration for 'Pedongi' being a case in point.

Many thanks to my wife, Veena, for encouraging me to write, not only as it kept me busy but also out of her hair. When discussing the chapters, her only refrain was to keep it simple so that it would appeal to a wider readership and not read like some stodgy, stilted Army manual. I've tried my best, but old habits die hard, and so, dear reader, many thanks for sticking with me till the last word.

Index